W9-CML-263

A Nation of HEROES

**Classic Inspirational Stories
from America's Favorite Magazine**

Reader's
Digest

THE READER'S DIGEST ASSOCIATION
PLEASANTVILLE, NEW YORK / MONTREAL

Acknowledgments

"Look What They've Done to Us" from *Newsweek*

"Mike's Flag" is condensed from a speech given by Leo K. Thorsness.

"Bravest Soldier I Ever Knew" by Edmund G. Love is condensed from *Army.*

"Abe Lincoln's Glorious Failure" from *A New Birth of Freedom: Abe Lincoln at Gettysburg*, copyright ©1983 by Philip B. Kunhardt, Jr., is published at $25 by Little, Brown & Company, 34 Beacon St., Boston, MA 02106

PROJECT STAFF

Senior Editor: Nancy Shuker
Designer: Jennifer R. Tokarski
Production Technology Manager: Douglas A. Croll
Administrative Assistant: Dina M. Fabry

READER'S DIGEST BOOKS

Editorial Director: Christopher Cavanaugh
Senior Design Director: Elizabeth L. Tunnicliffe
Director, Trade Publishing: Christopher T. Reggio
Vice President and General Manager: Harold Clarke

THE READER'S DIGEST ASSOCIATION, INC.

Editor-in-Chief: Eric W. Schrier
President, North America Books
 and Home Entertainment: Thomas D. Gardner

Library of Congress Cataloging in Publication Data has been applied for

ISBN 0-7621-8394-9

Address any comments about A NATION OF HEROES to:
 Editorial Director
 Reader's Digest Home Division
 Reader's Digest Road, Pleasantville, NY 10570-7000

To order additional copies of A NATION OF HEROES, call 1-800-846-2100.

For more Reader's Digest products and information, visit our website at rd.com

Printed in the United States of America

1 3 5 7 9 10 8 6 4 2

Contents

Introduction

The disastrous events on the morning of September 11, 2001, briefly knocked the breath out of the United States of America. We watched on live television as huge airliners purposely crashed into the World Trade Center towers. Then we listened in horror to reports of attacks on the Pentagon and the crash of yet a fourth hijacked passenger plane in Pennsylvania. We wondered how many other planes were headed for other targets, and what kinds of monsters could have orchestrated such staggering evil. That morning will live in our individual memories for our lifetimes, and in the national memory forever.

In the afternoon came grief and shock—thousands killed, symbols of our economic and military strength destroyed. We felt powerless over a mysterious and elusive enemy.

By the evening of the 11th, however, another side of the tragedy had emerged: stories of the brave firefighters, policemen, and EMTs who had risked and given their lives to save thousands of civilians; reports of the courageous passengers on flight 93 who had called husbands, wives, and parents to say a loving good-bye and then, as is the American way, voted to get out of their seats and stop the evil terrorists from hitting another target.

Another report told us about day-care workers who carried babies and toddlers over a mile to safety. Television let us see New York's Mayor Rudy Giuliani lead his city with an extraordinary mixture of compassion, grief, courage, and resolve. President Bush let us know that this horrible crime would not go unanswered and that the United States was committed to ending terrorism for this and all future generations.

When we went to bed that night of September 11, we felt many emotions: grief, fear, anger, and, yes, even rage. But we also had a sense that we, with God's help, were not powerless. With all of this evidence of ordinary people performing such heroic acts, we knew that together we would stand strong through this tragedy and get through the inevitable events to come—counter-attacks and war. Why? Because the true face of America had shone through once again and what we saw clearly was a nation full of heroes.

The heroic acts that followed the September 11 attacks reminded us here at Reader's Digest of the many inspiring stories of heroes that have appeared in our magazine over the years. We felt certain that reading these chronicles could only strengthen our readers' hope, patriotism, and resolve as together we struggle through these most trying of times. Each story in this book affirms that no matter what the challenge—even leveled build-ings with thousands of lives lost—the spirit of freedom will keep us together, resolved to defeat any foe.

We selected these articles because they reminded us of the kinds of selfless acts we saw and heard about on September 11 and in the days that followed. We hope that you will turn to this volume again and again over the next several months; if you begin to feel afraid or lose hope, read one of the stories. Your faith in mankind may be restored.

—The Editors

Giuliani leads the city out of darkness

Look What They've Done to Us

By Jonathan Alter
From *Newsweek*

The day after the blast Mayor Rudolph Giuliani was exhausted and grieving more than the public knew. Many of the uniformed officers he saw every day were dead. His staff, still barred from City Hall, looked like combat veterans. By midnight the mayor of New York had slipped back downtown to the ruins, where people worked all night, trying to find a trace of their friends and co-workers, now the nation's casualties of war.

Giuliani's mobilization of the city's emergency services was a marvel. But management alone wouldn't have created an aura had the mayor himself not been touched by fire, as he holed up in two places amid the onslaught.

The first was a fire department command post near the North Tower. Giuliani got a briefing on the evacuations from senior chiefs, even the most experienced of whom had no idea the burning towers would actually collapse.

Needing phone lines, Giuliani commandeered a Merrill Lynch office two blocks from the World Trade Center. After 45 minutes someone yelled, "Get down! It's coming down!"

The force of the South Tower collapse flattened the building across the street, and a huge plume of smoke blocked the exit the mayoral party needed. Giuliani, wearing a gas mask, was led running through a smoke-filled basement. "We tried one exit, it wouldn't open," he reported. "We tried the second exit, it wouldn't open. We went back upstairs and things were much worse. The windows had broken. It was dark, almost like nighttime. These clouds were rushing through the streets."

Giuliani's group found another exit in the basement, and they made it out through an adjoining building, where soot called "gray snow" was a foot deep. Except for a cell phone with sporadic connection, all contact with the outside world was cut.

Giuliani set off for a mile hike up Church Street, urging the ash-caked survivors to "Go north!" As the group walked, the second tower collapsed, sending another cloud of smoke and debris through the streets.

A frightened woman approached. The mayor touched her face and smiled. Farther up, a young rowdy got the mayoral "Shhhhhh!" he deserved. That set the tone. Giuliani was sensitive and tough and totally on top of everything.

Later, at a meeting, he was told it would take ten days to clean up one of the buildings. His response: "It took God seven days to create the earth. So we can do better than that, don't you think?"

Even in this cataclysm, which the mayor rightly called "the most difficult week in the history of New York," the city and the country found that most elusive of all democratic treasures—real leadership.

"It was," said one witness, "the finest thing I have ever seen, or hope to see, this side of heaven."

Legend of the Four Chaplains

By Lawrence Elliott

★ ★ ★

Friday, January 22, 1943. The ship tied up at the Army embarkation pier in New York Harbor was rusting through her battered gray paint. Soon she would be standing out to the North Atlantic, a bitter battleground that second winter of the war.

Once the *S.S. Dorchester* had been a luxury cruise liner, accommodating 314 cabin passengers in style, even opulence. Now, gutted and refitted, she had become a troop ship. That cheerless night, 524 soldiers trudged aboard to be berthed belowdecks in bunks stacked four-high. The trim little coastal steamer seemed too small and slow for the hazardous journey. But with Nazi submarines sinking Allied ships faster than they could be replaced, every available craft had been pressed into service.

Four Army chaplains—Fox, Goode, Poling, Washington— were aboard the *Dorchester*. For Lt. George Fox, it was the second time around.

George Lansing Fox is not old enough when President Wilson calls the nation to arms in the spring of 1917, but he tells officials he is 18, and they hand him a uniform. He is assigned to an ambulance company and serves through every major American campaign. Two days before the Armistice, Fox is caught in an artillery barrage. His back is riddled with shrapnel. The war is long over before he returns to his native Vermont, wearing a Silver Star, a Purple Heart and France's Croix de Guerre.

Fox gets a job as an accountant, but feels a call to preach and enrolls in a Bible Institute in Chicago. There he meets his future wife. They marry, move to Vermont and have two children. George Fox begins serving in the Methodist Church and, at 34, is ordained.

The next years are hard, but the Foxes get through them. George rides the circuit of half a dozen Vermont villages too small to afford their own pastor. He is content—until the Japanese attack Pearl Harbor.

Now past 40, Fox tells his wife, "I must go. I know what these boys are facing." He volunteers for the Corps of Chaplains.

Saturday, January 23. The *Dorchester* joined a convoy— freighters, troopships, tankers, naval escorts—steaming due east through the swelling gray-green sea. The ocean was not rough, but in the close confines of the overheated holds, where food, fuel and bilge smells were on permanent parade, those not already seasick were planning for it.

After seasickness, the most compelling preoccupation in the hold was guessing where the ship was bound. The rumor mill ground out destinations from Iceland to North Africa to the South Pacific. "Hey, come on, Rabbi," someone called to Lieutenant Goode. "Tell us where we're going." Pledged to secrecy, Goode replied, "What, and spoil the surprise?"

Three years to the day after the Armistice that ends World War I—November 11, 1921—a hush falls over Arlington National Cemetery. Ten-year-old Alexander David Goode stands at the edge of the crowd and watches as a soldier, killed in France, is laid to rest. No one knows his name. It doesn't matter; he is an American and he will forever memorialize America's war dead. Tears fill the young boy's eyes; his heart swells with love for his country.

> They were making for Torpedo Junction, the nickname for the dangerous waters off Newfoundland, where dozens of ships had been blasted to the bottom by German U-boats.

In high school Goode joins the National Guard and serves nine years, considering it his duty. His father is a rabbi, as was his father's father, and his father. Alex Goode becomes a rabbi too. He marries Teresa Flax, his childhood sweetheart, and when war comes he is leading the temple in York, Pa. Goode joins the Corps of Chaplains and puts in for overseas duty.

When his orders arrive, he has a brief last holiday in New York City with Teresa. Then he takes a ferry to Staten Island and reports aboard the *Dorchester*.

Saturday, January 30. At a fueling stop in St. John's, Newfoundland, the soldiers no longer doubted their destination. The *Dorchester* had docked there so often that everyone in town knew it was headed for Greenland. Even children shouted it out to them.

The *Dorchester* and two merchant ships sailed out of St. John's escorted by three Coast Guard cutters. Two patrolled the flanks; the third, the *Tampa*, was 3,000 yards out front. They were making for Torpedo Junction, the nickname for the dangerous waters off Newfoundland, where dozens of ships had been blasted to the bottom by German U-boats.

From this day on there would be repeated drills and alerts.

The chaplains noted that attendance at evening worship services was up sharply.

It turned bitterly cold. The sea rose, smashing against the ships. Ice began building up on the decks, slowing the *Dorchester* to ten knots. The men listened nervously as the bulkheads groaned and the steering chain clanked with every course correction.

The chaplains offered sympathy and dry crackers against an epidemic of seasickness. One sufferer said to Lieutenant Washington, "Listen, Father, if you really want to do good, get me out on deck so I can jump overboard." A few minutes later, the chaplain cajoled him into a game of cards.

For those still ambulatory, evening entertainment was music, wildly applauded, on bagpipes and guitar. Pfc. John Garey, playing the piano, attracted an ardent company of sing-alongs. Lieutenant Poling was an impresario, searching out talent, bolstering fading courage and joining earnestly in song.

The ships beat north through gale-force winds. Then, on Tuesday, the *Tampa*'s sonar detected the presence of a submarine, somewhere astern in the convoy's wash.

Clark Poling's family has a long tradition in the ministry, dating back seven generations. Clark grows up plain-spoken and sometimes brash. He tells his father, a noted clergyman and writer, that he is going to break the tradition and become a lawyer.

At Michigan's Hope College, Clark gets into plenty of mischief, and his marks are only mediocre. In his second year, he comes to his father and says, "Dad, I am going to preach. I can't deny the calling."

Clark enters Yale Divinity School, is ordained in 1938 and called to the First Reformed Church (Dutch) in Schenectady, N.Y. Everyone responds to him. The very exuberance that got him into trouble at school now wins hearts. Unbidden, he shows up at the doors of people who haven't been to church in years. "Hi," he says, "I'm Clark Poling, the new minister. Can you help me get started?"

When the war comes, Clark is married, has a two-year-old son and his wife is expecting another child. "Don't pray for my safe return," he tells his father. "Pray that I do my duty."

Tuesday, February 2. The *Tampa* dropped back and swept the periphery of the convoy, but failed to fix the sub's position. In the evening she returned to the patrol area up front, sharpening her evasive twists and turns. The other ships scrupulously followed.

Aboard the *Dorchester,* Capt. Hans J. Danielson ordered the men to sleep in their clothing, with life jackets close at hand. They were hard by the coast of Greenland, he said, only 150 miles from their destination. With daylight, there would be air cover from the American base.

The men returned to their bunks, subdued. A few wrote letters; others started a halfhearted poker game. But most men crawled onto their blankets and lay there staring.

Fear is catching, but so is laughter, and all four chaplains summoned it to pierce the gloom. Lieutenant Washington announced that God was prepared to forgive the poker players for raising the stakes from pennies to quarters. One soldier slyly asked him to bless his cards. The chaplain looked at the hand. "What?" he asked loudly. "Me bless a measly pair of deuces?"

The men began laughing; the tension broke.

John Washington is the first of seven children born to Irish-immigrant parents in Newark, N.J. The family doesn't have much, but the neighborhood is full of families just like theirs, people who join hands and march up to life's landmarks together—first Communions, illnesses, graduations. At age 12, John is stricken by a severe throat infection. When the doctors have done all they can, the parish priest administers the last rites. But John survives, and tells his sister, Anna, "God must have something special he wants me to do."

John becomes a Catholic priest and, in 1937, is assigned to

St. Stephen's in Arlington, N.J. He serves five happy years, but when the war comes, Father John applies at once for a chaplaincy. He now knows what God wants of him.

Wednesday, February 3. It was just after midnight, and the GIs were curled into their bunks. But few were asleep, and even fewer were wearing their clothes, despite the orders. Down in the hold it was just too hot.

John Garey came off guard duty, face and fingers stiff with cold. Hoping to get coffee, he went to the galley. He was there at 12:55 A.M., when a U-456 caught the *Dorchester* in its cross hairs.

Garey heard a distant thump and felt the deck lurch under his feet. "What's going on?" he yelled. The cook, who had been through it before, said, "We've been hit!" Garey ran for the deck.

Men were already pouring up out of the gangways, stunned and disoriented. The suffocating smell of ammonia from burst refrigeration pipes drifted out behind them.

The wound was mortal. The *Dorchester* took on water rapidly and began listing to starboard.

For all the practice alerts, nothing seemed to go right. Without power, the radio was silenced. No one thought to send up a distress flare, and the escort vessels pushed on into the darkness, unaware that the *Dorchester* was sinking. Overcrowded lifeboats capsized; rafts drifted away before anyone could reach them.

The men milled around on deck on the ragged edge of panic. Many came up from the hold without life jackets; others, wearing nothing but their underwear, felt the arctic blasts and knew they had only minutes to live.

The testimony of survivors tells us that the sole order in that ferment of struggling men, the only fragment of hope, came from the four chaplains, who suddenly appeared on the steeply sloping starboard side. Calmly they guided men to their boat stations. They opened a storage locker and distributed life jackets. Then they coaxed men, frozen with fear, over the side.

Pvt. William B. Bednar was floating in oil-smeared water, surrounded by debris and dead bodies, the ship looming over him. "I could hear men crying, pleading, praying, swearing," he recalled. "I could also hear the chaplains preaching courage." With his last strength Bednar swam out from under the ship and crawled aboard a life raft. "Their voices were the only thing that kept me going."

Coast Guard CPO John J. Mahoney realized he had forgotten his gloves and started back to his cabin. He was stopped by Chaplain Goode. "Never mind," Goode said. "I have two pairs."

Later, Mahoney realized the truth: a man preparing to abandon ship doesn't carry extra gloves. Rabbi Goode had already decided he wasn't leaving the *Dorchester*.

On the promenade deck, Second Engineer Grady Clark saw the chaplains coolly handing out life jackets from the locker until there were no more left. Then he watched in awe as they gave away their own.

By now the rail was awash, and Clark slipped into the frigid water. Looking back as he swam away, he saw the chaplains standing—their arms linked—braced against the slanting deck. They were praying.

Other men drew close. There were no more outcries, no panic, just words of prayer in Latin, Hebrew and English, addressed to the same God.

Then the stern came high out of the water, and the *Dorchester* slid down into the sea.

Of the 904 men aboard the troop carrier, 605 were lost. Those who lived will never forget the chaplains' heroism. Said John Ladd, one of the survivors: "It was the finest thing I have ever seen, or hope to see, this side of heaven."

By vote of Congress on January 18, 1961, a Special Medal of Heroism—the only one ever given—was posthumously awarded to the four chaplains. February 3 became Four Chaplains Observance Day, and in 1951, The Chapel of the Four Chaplains, an interfaith shrine, was dedicated in Philadelphia, with President Harry S. Truman in attendance and Daniel A. Poling, Clark's father, presiding.

More than half a century later, the legend of the four chaplains speaks to something deep in our hearts. For Father Washington didn't call out for a Catholic when he handed over his life jacket, nor Rabbi Goode for a Jew. They gave them to the next soldier in line—and then stood shoulder to shoulder in mutually supporting faith. This is the ideal of brotherhood. This is what we all want in America. This is what the four chaplains gave us.

A Medal for Roy Benavidez

By William A. Lowther

The White House, February 24, 1981, 12:55 P.M. President Reagan stands in front of the fireplace, with Sgt. Roy P. Benavidez, in uniform, to his right. "Can't we bring the family in here?" the President says. Benavidez's wife, Hilaria, steps forward with their three children.

"Nancy, Cap, come on," Reagan urges his wife and Secretary of Defense Casper W. Weinberger. Turning to the pool of reporters, the President says, "You are going to hear something you would not believe if it were a script. Wait until you hear the citation."

The citation, to be read by the President later at a Pentagon ceremony, describes Benavidez's "conspicuous gallantry in action at the risk of his life above and beyond the call of duty."

—From the notes of reporter Gilbert Lewthwaite,
Baltimore Sun

Loc Ninh, Vietnam, May 2, 1968, 1:30 P.M. The chaplain had spread a white altar cloth over the hood of a Jeep, and a small band of battle-weary American soldiers stood in a semicircle before it, their heads bowed in prayer. Among them was Sgt. Roy P. Benavidez. The son of a Texas sharecropper, he had enlisted in the Army 13 years before, at the age of 19, and was now a well-seasoned member of the Fifth Special Forces Group (Airborne).

The prayers were suddenly interrupted by helicopter pilots running by and the cries of chaos coming over the shortwave radio in a nearby tent: "Get us out of here. For God's sake, get us out!" The sound of automatic gunfire filled the background. "There was so much shooting," Benavidez said later, "it sounded like a popcorn machine."

Within moments a helicopter pilot was racing back to the takeoff pad. Benavidez, who was waiting for a mission assignment, ran after the pilot.

As the two men reached the pad, a helicopter was coming in, its fuselage bullet-ridden, a side door hanging open, with the gunner slumped forward. Benavidez eased him out and watched helplessly as the man died in his arms.

Screaming to be heard over the roar of the chopper's engines, Benavidez asked who was out there. A 12-man Special Forces team, he was told, one he had often worked with. Comrades. They had been dropped several hours before to check reports of enemy troop movement and had found themselves in the middle of a North Vietnamese army battalion.

A co-pilot, a crew chief and a replacement door gunner arrived to take the helicopter back for another rescue attempt. Benavidez climbed into the crew compartment. "What are you doing?" yelled the pilot. "I'm coming with you," replied Benavidez.

From the air they could see dozens of North Vietnamese foxholes pockmarking the area. Sniper platforms had been built at treetop level. Right in the middle were the Americans. They had formed a small circle in dense jungle cover, near a clearing where the helicopter was supposed to pick them up. Enemy soldiers were not more than 25 yards away at some points.

The chopper swooped low and was met by withering small-arms fire. It couldn't stay down long enough to get the team out. But there was another clearing about 75 yards away from which no enemy fire was coming.

"Over there, over there," Benavidez urged the pilot. When the chopper reached the clearing, it hovered about ten feet from the ground and Benavidez jumped.

He landed on his feet and started running. After covering about 20 yards, he was shot in the right leg. Bowled over by the bullet, he fell, but was up in an instant and kept moving.

"When you're shot, you feel a burning pain. Like you've been touched with hot metal," Benavidez recalled later. "But the fear that you experience is worse—and that's what keeps you going."

A hand grenade exploded in front of him. Shrapnel tore into his face, narrowly missing his eyes. Again he fell, and again he got up and ran. Bleeding profusely and in terrible pain, he staggered into the broken circle of his comrades, an unlikely-looking savior.

A Jungle Clearing, Vietnam, May 2, 1968, 2:15 P.M.
Benavidez found 8 of the 12 men still alive, all wounded. He told them to provide covering fire for the helicopter. When it swooped in again, he ordered the men out to meet it.

As they began moving, he spotted the body of the team leader. Dangling from the dead man's neck was a pouch containing classified papers with call signs and radio codes. It had to be recovered. He removed the pouch and slipped it into his shirt.

He pushed the men into the clearing. One had been hit in the face and had a bandage over his eyes. "Hang on to my neck," Benavidez ordered him. He half-carried another soldier, who had been shot in the legs. Another who had been hit in the stomach didn't want to move. Benavidez shouted and cursed and got all the wounded moving.

Under fire they reached the chopper, and Benavidez guided the men on board. Then he ran back to retrieve the body of the team leader—and was shot in the back. He pitched over in a somersault, landing flat on the ground. *O Lord, not here. Please, God, don't let me die here.* His head was filled with ringing bells. His body felt as if it was burning with fever. One leg seemed paralyzed.

At that moment, the helicopter pilot was killed. The chopper, which had been hovering just off the ground, crashed and tipped over. Benavidez rallied the survivors, including an injured door gunner, and led them back into the jungle. The other gunner had been killed, and the co-pilot, after freeing himself from the wreckage, joined Benavidez's group.

The men slumped down into a hollow. Wood flew everywhere as enemy bullets cut into the trees around them. A chorus of moaning and crying rose from this bloody band, and Benavidez, fearing the enemy would hear, ordered them to shut up. He opened a first-aid kit and gave several of them morphine. He gave himself two injections. Then he used the radio to direct air support from jets and gunships, hoping to suppress enemy fire long enough to allow another helicopter to land.

"Are you hit bad, sarge?" one of the men asked Benavidez.

"Hell, no," Benavidez drawled. "I been hit so many times I don't give a darn no more." Then one of the men was hit in the heel by a bullet, and Benavidez knew they had been spotted. It was get out now—or never.

"Please leave me here, sarge," one man pleaded. "I can't make it." While giving him first aid, Benavidez took another bullet in the thigh.

A helicopter arrived. Benavidez ordered everyone up. "We don't have permission to stay," he shouted. "We don't have permission to die. Pray and move out."

Under cover from the helicopter gunners, with the soldier wounded in the stomach on one side and the injured door gunner on the other, Benavidez staggered into the clearing. He put them aboard the chopper and went back for the others. As he bent over another wounded man, Benavidez was suddenly struck in the back of the head by a rifle butt.

He fell, but instinctively rolled over and bounced to his feet. He stood facing a North Vietnamese soldier, who rushed at him with his bayonet. Benavidez grabbed it, cutting his hand wide open. While pulling the soldier toward him, he drew out his belt knife with his other hand and stabbed him.

Now he was covered with blood, hurting badly and screaming, and beginning to lose his sense. Most of his men were up and moving. Somehow summoning a last reserve of strength, Benavidez picked up two of the weaker ones and started toward the chopper. As he drew near, he saw two enemy soldiers crawling toward the chopper where the door gunners couldn't see them. He scooped up a nearby rifle and shot both. One of the door gunners, confused by what was happening, swung his gun around at Benavidez, thinking the sergeant was a North Vietnamese soldier who was shooting at him. The pilot shouted to the gunner just in time.

After getting the men on board, Benavidez made one last sweep of the perimeter, looking for injured soldiers and classified material. Finally, he pulled himself aboard and passed out.

When the helicopter put down at Loc Ninh, a doctor took one look and said, "There's nothing I can do for him."

Benavidez heard the words, opened his eyes and, unable to speak, defiantly spit at the doctor.

The Congress, November 21, 1980, 1:30 P.M. The House Military Personnel Subcommittee considered a bill to exempt Roy Benavidez from the time limit on awarding medals for heroism.

Benavidez had received the Distinguished Service Cross, the nation's second-highest award for valor, in 1968. But five years later, when Lt. Col. Ralph R. Drake, the Special Forces mission commander, learned more details of Benavidez's actions, he decided to recommend him for the highest award, the Medal of Honor. The recommendation was at first rejected for lack of new and substantive information, and by the time that became available, the time limit on Medals of Honor had expired. A Texas congressman and an Army representative appealed to Congress to make an exception.

Maj. Robert Roush, formerly of the Army's Military Awards Branch, testified: "I must stress that Sergeant Benavidez voluntarily joined his comrades, who were in critical straits. He constantly exposed himself to withering fire, and his refusal to be stopped, despite numerous severe wounds, saved the lives of at least eight men."

The Pentagon, February 24, 1981, 1:45 P.M. Roy P. Benavidez approaches the podium in the courtyard, his stocky frame shuddering from the dull ache in his back, his legacy of war. He extends a bayonet-scarred hand to his commander in chief.

"There I was, a little old Texas farm boy, with the President," Benavidez said later.

The President speaks:

"Several years ago, we brought home a group of American fighting men who had obeyed their country's call and who fought as bravely and as well as any Americans in our history.

"An individual brought up on a farm outside of Cuero, Texas, is here today. His story has been overlooked or buried for several years.

"Secretary Weinberger, would you please escort Sergeant Benavidez forward." The President drapes the blue ribbon around the soldier's neck and hugs him. Roy Benavidez, retired since 1976 on 80 percent medical disability, stands proud and erect, his dark eyes clouding with emotion.

"Sergeant Benavidez," the President continues, "a nation grateful to you, and to all your comrades living and dead, awards you its highest symbol of gratitude for service above and beyond the call of duty, the Medal of Honor."

There's a Girl
on the Tracks!

By Warren R. Young

I t was a moment frozen in time by terror. Nearly 100 people waiting on the subway platform beneath New York's 86th Street and Lexington Avenue stood transfixed. A few screamed, but they could barely be heard. For, thundering into the station at 30 m.p.h. was a heavily laden, rush-hour train—a million pounds of screeching stainless steel and fateful momentum. And in its path, the onlookers could see a young man, his face pale with concentration, trying to jump up from the tracks four feet below.

With terrible certainty, they could see that he was not likely to make it. The train was hurtling toward him, ponderously swaying to within an inch or two of the metal-capped edge of the platform, like a gargantuan sausage slicer. The man's first jump carried him only high enough for his chest to strike the edge of the platform, and he fell back to the track.

Now the train was merely feet away. He gathered himself for one last desperate attempt. Then he felt himself rising, and it seemed just possible after all that at least his torso might get clear. But the last thought he had before the train reached the spot was "There go my legs!"

Less than two minutes earlier, 34-year-old Everett Sanderson, an unemployed musician, had been on his way home after visiting his mother. It was 5:10 P.M., January 16, 1975, and around him swirled the normal evening bustle, as people hurried down from the city's streets or up the stairs from the express-train level below. About every 2½ minutes, at this time of day, another local train came through, and one of them had left half a minute before.

At this moment, chance was guiding several strangers—and one particular train—each on a path that would soon converge with Everett's. Changing from express to local was 20-year-old Miguel Maisonett, a slender, clean-cut black youth sporting a neat Afro hairdo. Miguel was deep in thought about his future. He had just collected his final paycheck as a city health-department rat inspector; his job had been eliminated because of spending cutbacks. Ever since age 15, when he had dropped out of school to support himself and his younger brother (who had continued through high school and was now in college), Miguel had managed; but now jobs were scarce.

Approaching the stairs leading up to the same uptown-local platform was Transit patrolman Rex Johnson, on his beat. Coming through the turnstiles was Mrs. Joanna DeJesus, whose right eye was bandaged from a recent operation. With her were her button-cute, four-year-old daughter, Michelle, and Mrs. DeJesus's sister, Margarita Esquilin.

Half a mile to the south at 77th Street, in the front cab of his train, 60-year-old motorman Daniel Miller had just released the brakes in response to a green "all-clear-ahead" signal light. Now he swung the master-controller handle to the "power" position, sending 600 volts of direct current into the 40 electric motors hooked to the train's 40 axles. The 70-second run through the tunnel to 86th Street had begun.

The DeJesus trio moved through the thickening crowd and stopped about two feet from the bright yellow stripe painted along the platform's steel-capped edge. Just then, Michelle wriggled her hand free from her mother's, hopped toward the edge to look for the train—but slipped and fell onto the tracks. The screams and shouts for help began: "There's a girl on the tracks!" "Somebody save her!" "Save her!" All Mrs. DeJesus could see was the bright-red coat and motionless form of her child, face down on the wooden ties with her feet across the nearest rail.

Everett and Miguel, 85 feet apart, each stepped to the platform's edge to see what had happened. Everett was about 35 feet uptown from the center of the commotion, Miguel 50 feet below. Both could see the helpless figure on the tracks. And both expected somebody in the crowd to jump down and pick up the stunned child.

Fifteen seconds passed. The crowd felt a gush of wind caused by the oncoming train, then heard the first distant grumble as it barreled through the rock-walled tunnel toward them. Down on the tracks, Michelle began to rouse. Her eyes tightly closed, she cried, "Mommy! Mommy!"

But he had never run in conditions like these, dressed in a heavy jacket, down in the trough of a subway— and with a little girl's life at stake.

The shouts for somebody to save the little girl kept up, but nobody moved. Ten more seconds ticked by—it was almost half a minute since the fall. Then Everett, his own son in the custody of his ex-wife, asked himself, "What if it was *my* child down there?" And in a jumble of gallantry and foolhardiness, he jumped down to the tracks and started running.

Years ago, as an Ohio schoolboy, Everett had played football and basketball and once, at a track meet, had carried off all the awards. But he had never run in conditions like these, dressed in a heavy jacket, down in the trough of a subway—and with a little girl's life at stake.

On the other side of the crowd, Miguel, too, had decided to try to save the girl. Unlike Everett, however, he was thoroughly familiar with the tracks, for as a boy he and his friends, in a dare devil game, used to jump down and run across them between trains. Now, he leaped down and began sprinting.

By the time Miguel had run ten feet, he could hear the sound of the train swelling hugely in the tunnel behind him. He knew that it would reach the station in seconds. But then he saw the other man running toward him, closer to Michelle

> **Because of this incline, Miller could neither see Officer Johnson's warning flashlight nor yet peer into the station to spot any trouble.**

and with a better chance of reaching her. With an easy vault perfected by years of boyhood practice, Miguel swung his body up onto the platform.

By this time, Officer Johnson was up the stairs and aware of the desperate situation. He knew there was no way to cut off the power from the station, nor any fast way for him to contact the train to stop it. Headlight flashes flickered in the dark tunnel, and the noise level rose. Facing the unseen train and waving his flashlight from side to side, as regulation prescribed for an emergency, the six-foot-three-inch, 200-pound officer began running backward, shouting, "Stand clear! Get back, everybody!" The train would reach the station in about ten seconds.

Motorman Miller, at this point, had been pouring power into the 4000-horsepower electric motors to carry the train up and over a steep little slope in front of the 86th Street station. Because of this incline, Miller could neither see Officer Johnson's warning flashlight nor yet peer into the station to spot any trouble. Near the station entrance, he cut off the power. Normally, the train would be allowed to coast far into the station, then gradually be braked.

Miller's 25 years of bringing subway trains into stations had taught him never to be surprised to see objects in his train's path. Usually, they were unimportant. Newspapers blowing along the rails were commonplace. Once in a while, however, an "object" might be human—two or three suicides had jumped to their deaths under his wheels, waiting until the last instant when he could do nothing, And, once, a drunk on the tracks was saved by Miller's quick stop. So now, as always, his right hand was firmly wrapped around the brake lever.

Everett was so busy running that he never saw Miguel hop down and back up, nor did he notice Officer Johnson waving his light. All his thoughts were focused on the girl. She was still 20 feet away when he suddenly felt the asphalt tremble. Two brilliant headlights glared in his eyes as the front of the train, 12 feet tall and 9 feet wide, abruptly filled the mouth of the tunnel.

The 240 feet now separating the train from little Michelle looked like far less to Everett, as the monster rumbled toward him still going almost 30 m.p.h., or 44 feet every second. Everett could see the motorman, his expressionless face giving no sign that he saw any-body on the track, looking even more remote because he was so far up—his feet, like those of the people on the platform, were about at Everett's eye level. Everett kept running.

With a sinking feeling, he thought the first car must have caught Everett's legs and pulled him under.

Sometime during the first two seconds after the train entered the station, Motorman Miller spotted the child and the man on the tracks. He slammed the brake handle into "Emergency Stop," locking all the train's wheels. Sparks flew like fireworks as they skidded, grinding their metal against the rails with a tortured screech. Immediately, the train slowed, but it would still pass the spot where Michelle lay in only five seconds!

Everett was only a step from Michelle. In the train cab, Motorman Miller silently prayed, "Oh, God, I hope I don't hit them!" On the platform, Miguel was also in the path of the train, kneeling and leaning over the edge toward Everett with out-stretched arms. With three seconds to go, Everett seized Michelle in his right hand and, possessed of a strength he never knew he had, hurled her into Miguel's waiting arms. The impact knocked Miguel onto his back, with the child sprawled on his chest, safe at last.

For the first time, Everett recognized his own predicament. The train's speed had by this time been cut in half—to 16 m.p.h., or some 24 feet per second—but it was 40 feet away. There were two seconds to go.

Everett placed his hands on the edge of the platform, jumped for his life—and failed. By now, there was a single second left before the train would pass the spot where he was. Everett got ready for one last, desperate jump. Then, with the train so close that its mammoth bulk seemed virtually on top of him, he felt himself rising like an elevator. Hands belonging to Officer Johnson, Michelle's Aunt Margarita, and Miguel were lifting him by the jacket and his arms. Everett hoped that his torso would clear the train, but he felt sure his legs would be amputated.

As the train passed, Motorman Miller lost sight of Everett. With a sinking feeling, he thought the first car must have caught Everett's legs and pulled him under. But he was puzzled by the absence of the familiar, sickening *thud* he always heard when a train passed over the body of a suicide. For more than three seconds, the train kept skidding, Finally, it stopped, 26 feet beyond where Everett and Michelle had been. Miller stepped out on the platform to see what had happened.

A pile of human figures on the platform were struggling to their feet. The three rescuers had tugged so mightily on Everett that some of them fell—with Everett, unharmed, landing among them. (Later, he would find a mark made by the train on the edge of his right shoe.) For the next few minutes, while Motorman Miller and Officer Johnson made sure of the happy outcome, the crowd patted Everett on the back and kept telling him he was a hero. At last, everybody went on about his business—Miguel went home in a taxi, Mrs. DeJesus took another cab to the hospital to make sure Michelle was not really hurt, Officer Johnson resumed his beat, and Motorman Miller announced that the train would continue its regular run. Everett Sanderson got on the train, too, and rode it to his stop.

The grateful New York Transit Authority presented Everett and Miguel with medals for civilian heroism, plus a five-year pass for free subway travel for Miguel and a lifetime pass for Everett. Miguel found a job in the mailroom of the Transit Authority. Everett, for his part, decided to pursue a new career, in the nutrition field, and trained for it, riding the subway to class. In addition, he was presented the prestigious bronze lifesaving medal of the Carnegie Hero Fund Commission and a $1,000 check.

"I don't know whether this has changed my life," says Everett. "I know it almost ended it. But if I hadn't tried to save that little girl, if I had just stood there like the others, I would have died inside. I would have been no good to myself from then on."

This grimy rag became our symbol of freedom

Mike's Flag

CONDENSED FROM A SPEECH BY
LEO K. THORSNESS, MEDAL OF HONOR WINNER
AND WASHINGTON STATE SENATOR

Y ou've probably seen the bumper sticker somewhere along the road. It depicts an American flag, accompanied by the words, "These colors don't run." I'm always glad to see this, because it reminds me of an incident from my confinement in North Vietnam at the Hoa Lo P.O.W. camp, or the Hanoi Hilton, as it became known. Then a major in the U.S. Air Force, I had been captured and imprisoned from 1967 to 1973.

Our treatment had been frequently brutal. After three years, however, the beatings and torture became less frequent. During the last year, we were allowed outside most days to bathe. We showered by drawing water from a concrete tank with a home-made bucket.

One day as we all stood by the tank, stripped of our clothes, a young naval pilot named Mike Campbell found the remnants of a handkerchief in a gutter that ran under the prison wall. Mike managed to sneak the grimy rag into our cell and began fashioning it into a flag. Over time we all loaned him a little soap and he spent days cleaning the material. We helped by scrounging and stealing bits and pieces of anything he could use.

At night, under his mosquito net, Mike worked on the flag. He made red and blue from ground-up roof tiles and tiny amounts of ink, and painted the colors onto the cloth with watery rice glue. Using thread from his one blanket and a homemade bamboo needle, he sewed on stars.

Early in the morning a few days later—when the guards were not alert—he whispered loudly from the back of our cell, "Hey gang, look here." He proudly held up this tattered piece of cloth, waving it as if in a breeze.

If you used your imagination, you could tell it was supposed to be an American flag. When he raised that smudgy fabric, we automatically stood straight and saluted, our chests puffing out, and more than a few eyes had tears.

About once a week the guards would strip us, run us outside and go through our clothing. During one of these shakedowns, they found Mike's flag. We all knew what would happen.

That night they came for him. Night interrogations were always the worst. They opened the cell door and pulled Mike out. We could hear the beginning of the torture before they even had him in the torture cell. They beat him most of the night. About daylight they pushed what was left of him back through the cell door. He was badly broken; even his voice was gone.

Within two weeks, despite the danger, Mike scrounged another piece of cloth and began another flag. The Stars and Stripes, our national symbol, was worth the sacrifice to him.

Now, whenever I see the flag, I think of Mike and the morning he first waved that tattered emblem of a nation. It was then, thousands of miles from home in a lonely prison cell, that he showed us what it is to be truly free.

Some sacrificed their lives, some their health. But all of them sacrificed time they could never make up

They Did What Had to Be Done

By Ralph Kinney Bennett

When I was a boy, fascinated by war and soldiering, I fought many a campaign in the woods and fields along Lynn Run Creek in Rector, Pa. The Revolution, the Indian Wars, the Civil War, both World Wars—all were fought with carved wooden rifles and heroic élan until the inevitable armistices of dinner or bedtime.

In the rural Ligonier Valley, I seldom saw real soldiers except for Pennsylvania National Guardsmen, who marched in holiday parades. But I didn't take these men seriously as soldiers. After all, my brother Richard and his pals were among those marching.

I did pay special attention to veterans, because they had once been real soldiers. Still, I was a little disappointed. Many of them had served in the "Big One," as they called the First World War. Now they were gray-haired or balding guys who pulled on old olive-drab tunics they could barely button. I just couldn't quite see them charging through Belleau Wood with fixed bayonets.

31

There was no Veterans Day back then. It was called Armistice Day. We school kids would pause at 11 A.M. to "remember the 11s," as I called it. We'd pledge allegiance and stand in silence to remember those who had served and died in the First World War, which had ended at the "11th hour of the 11th day of the 11th month," November 11, 1918. I would stand, eyes closed, picturing explosions and barbed wire and men in flat tin hats pouring out of trenches into "no man's land."

I made no connection between those images and the men I saw around me every day: the wiry, bespectacled man down the road who spoke with gravel in his voice because he had been gassed on the Western Front in 1918; the men named Keffer and Murdock, Breniser and Hamill whom I saw in the stores and streets of Ligonier, all of whom were World War I vets. As members of the American Legion, Veterans of Foreign Wars and other groups, they provided honor guards or marched in parades, grinning at relatives and friends, shuffling from time to time to pick up the lost cadence of long ago.

World War II was fresher in my memory. The "vet" I observed most closely was Uncle Robert, who had been captured in 1943 by the Germans in North Africa and spent the rest of the war in prison camps. He returned nervous and given to nightmares. He chain-smoked and drank a good bit. I never heard him talk about the war. He seemed to want to put the military experience as far behind him as he could.

As the years passed, the other men who had come home moved quickly back into civilian life. I was always a little surprised to see someone I knew only as mailman, plumber or barber squeezed into an old uniform, wearing an American Legion cap and carrying a rifle or the flag. Paunches protruded over belts; faces were often red with exertion from the short march down Main Street.

Somehow I got it in my head that these men had just put in time in uniform. They couldn't have been the helmeted figures I had seen in newsreels hunched by the sea wall at Tarawa or in the hedgerows of Normandy. These were just guys who liked to shoot the breeze and get a couple of beers "down at the Vets."

One day when I was 12, I was in Dr. Harold Kinney's office to be treated for a foot injury. In the ignorance of youth I repeated something I had overheard: that vets were mainly blowhards who had never been near the "real war." I said something about all those guys in the parades being "cooks and bottle-washers."

Doc Kinney had sad, worldly-wise eyes and a slightly jowly look that reminded me of a bloodhound. He leaned back against a table filled with books and medical instruments, folded his arms and looked at me with those sad eyes.

"Listen," he said in his low, raspy voice. "You should respect every veteran. You know why?" There was a long pause. I sat looking down at my bandaged foot, embarrassed. "Because they were there," Doc said. "They'd rather have been here. But they did what had to be done."

He turned and put some bandages in a jar. "We're not all Alvin Carey," he said, referring to a Valley boy who had won the Medal of Honor in France. "But any of the men you see around here might have been.

"You're just a kid," Doc continued. "You don't know what a year is, let alone two or three, taken out of your life." He cracked a half-smile and patted me on the back as I left the office.

When Doc spoke those words, "there" was Korea and Occupied Germany. By the time I was married, "there" was Vietnam. And once again men were doing what had to be done. Some would never return. Those who did would march in other parades or provide color guards for sparsely attended Veterans Day ceremonies.

I never forgot the words Doc said to me that day. And whenever I see veterans, I don't ask whether they were manning a machine gun or clerking in a supply depot. I just think to myself that while I grew up, went to school, raised a family, enjoyed the fruits and freedoms of the freest nation on earth, they were "there." They did what had to be done. Some sacrificed their lives, some their health. But all of them sacrificed time they could never make up.

Not long ago, I walked up the hill at Ligonier Valley Cemetery. The rows of graves look down on the Loyalhanna Creek and beyond it, to the tree-shaded town. I drank in the beauty of it all—the flag waving over the square, the clock on the Methodist church, the school on the hill. Then I made a special point of going to two gravestones.

The first one is inscribed simply: *Alvin P. Carey, 1916-1944, S/Sgt. 38 Inf 2nd Div.* When Alvin Carey's machine-gun unit was pinned down near Plougastel, France, on a hot August day some 50 years ago, he gathered as many grenades as he could and advanced alone 200 yards up a hill in the face of intense enemy fire. Despite mortal wounds, he destroyed a German pillbox, saving the lives of his men and allowing the position to be taken.

They tell me Alvin Carey was a stocky country boy, quiet and unassuming, just as ordinary a guy as anyone you might see hunting on Chestnut Ridge or shopping at the hardware store. But on that August day, he did what had to be done.

Then I walked to another gravestone. It reads *Harold J. Kinney, 1909-1969, M.D., Maj. USA WWII.* I looked around at the acres of stones on that hill. Over the years, the veterans groups have come and diligently placed small bronze flagholders at every veteran's grave. From one end of the cemetery to the other, hundreds of flags waved in the sunlight.

"Well, Doc, there sure are a lot of 'em," I said. Tears came to my eyes. I thought to myself: God bless every veteran. The ones at peace here. The ones I see marching in the next parade. The ones I pass unknowing on the street. From Yorktown to Gettysburg, from Plougastel to the Persian Gulf, they were there. They did what had to be done.

He was a street-hardened brawler who
murdered the English language with aplomb.
He was also the …

Bravest Soldier I Ever Knew

BY EDMUND G. LOVE
CONDENSED FROM *ARMY*

T he question most frequently asked of me as a combat
historian in World War II is, "Who was the bravest soldier you ever knew?" The answer is easy: Artie Klein.
Artie stood 5 feet, 11 inches tall and had narrow shoulders
and narrow hips. The beginnings of a beer belly bulged out over
his belt. He had wide, soft-brown eyes and a skeptical smile. He
walked with small but deliberate steps and wore his cap perched
over his right eyebrow, the way a tough would wear it. And Artie
Klein *was* tough.

He was born in the Williamsburg section of Brooklyn, N.Y.,
the son of immigrants. Shortly before World War I, Artie's father
joined the New York National Guard and served in France with
the 106th Infantry, a Brooklyn regiment. The older Klein was
promoted to sergeant, an honor of great magnitude for an immi-
grant Jew. Proud of those stripes and grateful to his country, he
stayed in the Army for 20 years, moving from post to post, spending furloughs with his wife and son in the little flat under the
Williamsburg Bridge.

One result of his long absences from home was a son who was largely undisciplined. Artie was a leader of street gangs, a brawler devoted to petty crime. When it became apparent that he was going to be sent to reform school, he lied about his age and joined the U.S. Army. He was 14 years old.

Artie served undistinguished tours in China, the Philippines, Hawaii and Panama. He knew every dive from Shanghai to New York City. In 16 years he never rose above the rank of private, a grave disappointment to his father. At the time of Pearl Harbor, he was stationed at Fort Benning, Ga. A few days after war was declared, Artie was promoted to sergeant and put to work drilling recruits.

He was not enchanted. The stripes cramped his style, but the news of his promotion pleased his father so much that Artie decided to go along with the gag, as he put it. He had absorbed enough knowledge to hold his rank instinctively. He was an expert on every infantry weapon and had a flair for teaching, although his favorite phrase was, "Now youse men listen to me."

In 1942, desperate for officers, the Army sent all top sergeants at Benning to Officer Candidate Schools. Artie was commissioned a second lieutenant and put in charge of weapons instruction at the Infantry School.

News of this came shortly before Artie's father died of cancer and he got out of bed and marched down to Governor's Island to ask one last favor of an old friend: that Artie be assigned to *his* old regiment, the 106th Infantry, stationed in Hawaii.

Artie Klein was irked to find himself in the 106th Infantry. The colonel in charge was a West Pointer who had no love for soldiers of Artie's type. To him, Artie was the kind of guy more at home in a sleazy bar than in an officers club.

But there was one good thing. Many of the enlisted men in the 1st Battalion, to which Klein was assigned, also came from the Williamsburg section of Brooklyn. They murdered the English language with the same aplomb. Some had even belonged to street gangs. Artie knew how to handle them. After a long day, he would take off his uniform and join them for a game of craps at some hidden location. There also was something indomitable about him that soon won the devotion of every man in the battalion. They sensed that he was still an enlisted man at heart.

Artie certainly did nothing socially to endear himself to the other officers in the regiment. In the officers club he might have passed as the bouncer, but never as a member. His whole attitude suggested he was ready to fight his way inside.

The 106th Infantry received its baptism of fire at Eniwetok on February 19, 1944. Baker Company, of which Klein was weapons platoon commander, landed in the first wave. The Japanese sank many of the U.S. landing craft before they reached the beach. In the swirling, smoke-filled, fiery melee, the first waves dissolved into little islands of beleaguered men stalled a few feet from the water's edge.

Landing with his platoon, Klein took charge. Through the heavy enemy fire, he moved all over the beach, putting separated squads and platoons back together and leading attacks that wiped out the nearest enemy positions.

In the first two hours Klein's platoon sergeant, his radio operator and his runner were killed within inches of him, but he kept moving about without regard to what was likely to happen to him.

At one point, the Japanese launched a massive counterattack. Slowly, then in increasing numbers, the American troops, still relatively green in battle, began to give up their positions and move back toward the beach. Klein realized immediately what was happening. He looked around, found a small hillock and climbed onto it.

He could be seen quite plainly by virtually everyone within his area, including the enemy. He began waving his carbine at first one American and then another.

"I'll shoot the first son of a bitch that takes another step backward," he yelled. "Youse bastards are supposed to be all-

American soldiers. Now let's see youse show a little guts."

The troops stopped where they were, looked up at Klein, and turned around. The counterattack ended a few minutes later.

He brought order out of chaos on that beach, but more important, his calmness and courage marked his men. From that morning on, the 1st Battalion, 106th Infantry, was molded in Artie Klein's image. It soon became known as one of the finest infantry units in the Pacific.

After the 106th returned to Hawaii, an Army magazine ran an article about Klein's exploits under the title, "The One-Man Army—Klein." As a result, Klein was stuck with the nickname "Omak," which he bore for the rest of the war. In May 1944, he was awarded the Bronze Star.

Klein's battalion commander collected 52 affidavits from the men and submitted a recommendation for the Medal of Honor. But the recommendation was turned down—in my opinion, by the officers who had run into Klein at one time or another in the officers clubs.

"What the hell difference does it make?" he said later to a friend. "Someday, after I'm dead, somebody will plant a tree for me on the Staten Island Ferry. Then everybody will put cigarette butts in it. It don't mean nothing."

On June 1, the 27th Division sailed for Saipan. Artie Klein's regiment followed shortly. He was now executive officer of Baker Company.

The last paragraph of the Army article on Artie Klein said, "If One-Man-Army Klein ever goes into combat again, he probably will not live for more than ten minutes."

Klein lasted 30 minutes at Saipan. He was cut down by Japanese machine-gun fire after deliberately exposing himself so that his men could advance.

It was said that he would never walk again, and on three different occasions he was ordered back to the States. He successfully fought these orders. While Artie was hospitalized, President

Roosevelt came and personally pinned the Distinguished Service Cross on his pajamas for the action at Eniwetok.

"You see that hand?" he said when I visited him. "You know who shook it? The President of the United States, that's who. What the hell do you think my old man would say if he knew that? Just think, the President shook hands with a no-good bum like me."

Artie Klein reported back to duty with Baker Company late in October 1944. He limped off the plane at Espiritu Santo just three days after his discharge from the hospital. On the day before he was to leave Espiritu Santo, he gave a friend headed back to the States a handkerchief to take to Klein's mother in Brooklyn.

Wrapped in the handkerchief were the medals Artie had won—the Distinguished Service Cross, Silver Star, Bronze Star and two Purple Hearts—and a set of his captain's bars. "I think maybe she ought to take them down to the cemetery and show them to my old man," Artie said. "I think he'd like to know."

"That's when I knew I'd never see Omak again," the friend said later.

The 27th Division went into the attack on Okinawa on the morning of April 19, 1945. To take a key ridge it was necessary to send a rifle company along the face of a sheer cliff to clear out cave and pillbox positions. Baker Company was chosen for the task.

At dawn, with Klein in the lead, the troops moved out. For two days, sometimes clinging to rocks or bushes, at other times moving hand over hand, they scrambled along. In the end they wiped out a whole Japanese battalion. (The Tenth Army commander later characterized this movement along the escarpment as the most masterful infantry action he had ever seen.)

In the mop-up, one Japanese position still held out, atop a pinnacle 50 yards to the front. "Somebody's going to have to go after that rock," Klein said.

"Artie," his executive officer said, "anybody who goes after that rock is a dead man."

Klein smiled and nodded. "I'll take it. You get everybody ready and move in when I signal."

Klein borrowed an automatic rifle and six grenades. No martyr, he moved from rock to rock, never giving the enemy a good target.

Somehow he got within five yards of the pinnacle's base. He pulled the pin on a grenade, straightened up and threw.

The enemy was ready. Four or five of them showed themselves and fired. Every man in Baker Company was ready too. The Japanese soldiers were cut to pieces. Baker Company cheered, then looked for Artie Klein.

He was sitting at the base of the rock. Twice he tried to get up only to sink back again. Then he slowly rolled over on his side and was still. His executive officer radioed the regiment.

"You can move the Third Battalion in now," he said. "Colonel—Artie Klein is dead. He was a good man, colonel. So help me, I never saw a better one."

When they brought Klein's body out, they found 24 bullet wounds in it. He must have suffered most of those wounds before throwing that last grenade.

Artie Klein was buried with full military honors in the 27th Division cemetery on Okinawa. When I visited his grave, his battered helmet still hung from a point of the Star of David. After Okinawa, Klein was again recommended for the Medal of Honor, the only man I ever knew who was recommended twice for it. No one followed up on it and he was presented posthumously with something less.

Artie Klein is long forgotten now. Some years ago, I went to his father's grave in Brooklyn. A set of sergeant's stripes were painted on each side of this inscription: "Anything is possible in this country."

They were just kids, but they
understood the secret of freedom

A Mason-Dixon Memory

By Clifton Davis

★ ★ ★

Dondré Green glanced uneasily at the civic leaders and
sports figures filling the hotel ballroom in Cleveland.
They had come from across the nation to attend a
fund-raiser for the National Minority College Golf Scholarship
Foundation. I was the banquet's featured entertainer. Dondré, an
18-year-old high-school senior from Monroe, La., was the
evening's honored guest.

"Nervous?" I asked the handsome young man in his starched
white shirt and rented tuxedo.

"A little," he whispered, grinning.

One month earlier, Dondré had been just one more black
student attending a predominantly white Southern school.
Although most of his friends and classmates were white, Dondré's
race had never been an issue. Then, on April 17, 1991, Dondré's
black skin provoked an incident that made nationwide news.

"Ladies and gentlemen," the emcee said, "our special guest,
Dondré Green."

As the audience stood applauding, Dondré walked to the
microphone and began his story. "I love golf," he said quietly.

"For the past two years, I've been a member of the St. Frederick High School golf team. And though I was the only black member, I've always felt at home playing at the mostly white country clubs across Louisiana."

The audience leaned forward; even the waiters and busboys stopped to listen. As I listened, a memory buried in my heart since childhood began fighting its way to life.

"If we leave, we forfeit this tournament. If we stay, Dondré can't play."

"Our team had driven from Monroe," Dondré continued. "When we arrived at the Caldwell Parish Country Club in Columbia, we walked to the putting green."

Dondré and his teammates were too absorbed to notice the conversation between a man and St. Frederick athletic director James Murphy. After disappearing into the clubhouse, Murphy returned to his players.

"I want to see the seniors," he said. "On the double!" His face seemed strained as he gathered the four students, including Dondré.

"I don't know how to tell you this," he said, "but the Caldwell Parish Country Club is reserved for whites only." Murphy paused and looked at Dondré. His teammates glanced at each other in disbelief. "I want you seniors to decide what our response should be," Murphy continued. "If we leave, we forfeit this tournament. If we stay, Dondré can't play."

As I listened, my own childhood memory from 32 years ago broke free.

In 1959 I was 13 years old, a poor black kid living with my mother and stepfather in a small black ghetto on Long Island, N.Y. My mother worked nights in a hospital, and my stepfather drove a coal truck. Needless to say, our standard of living was somewhat short of the American dream.

Nevertheless, when my eighth-grade teacher announced a

graduation trip to Washington, D.C., it never crossed my mind
that I would be left behind. Besides a complete tour of the
nation's capital, we would visit Glen Echo Amusement Park in
Maryland. In my imagination, Glen Echo was Disneyland,
Knott's Berry Farm and Magic Mountain rolled into one.

My heart beating wildly, I raced home to deliver the mimeo-
graphed letter describing the journey. But when my mother saw
how much the trip would cost, she just shook her head. We
couldn't afford it.

After feeling sad for ten seconds, I decided to try to fund the
trip myself. For the next eight weeks, I sold candy bars door-to-
door, delivered newspapers and mowed lawns. Three days before
the deadline, I'd made just barely enough. I was going!

The day of the trip, trembling with excitement, I climbed
onto the train. I was the only nonwhite in our section.

Our hotel was not far from the White House. My roommate
was Frank Miller, the son of a businessman. Leaning together out
of our window and dropping water balloons on passing tourists
quickly cemented our new friendship.

Every morning, almost a hundred of us loaded noisily onto
our bus for another adventure. We sang our school fight song
dozens of times—en route to Arlington National Cemetery and
even on an afternoon cruise down the Potomac River.

We visited the Lincoln Memorial twice, once in daylight, the
second time at dusk. My classmates and I fell silent as we walked
in the shadows of those 36 marble columns, one for every state in
the Union that Lincoln labored to preserve. I stood next to Frank
at the base of the 19-foot seated statue. Spotlights made the white
Georgian marble seem to glow. Together, we read those famous
words from Lincoln's speech at Gettysburg, remembering the
most bloody battle in the War between the States: ". . . *we here
highly resolve that these dead shall not have died in vain—that this
nation, under God, shall have a new birth of freedom . . .*"

As Frank motioned me into place to take my picture, I took

one last look at Lincoln's face. He seemed alive and so terribly sad.

The next morning I understood a little better why he wasn't smiling. "Clifton," a chaperone said, "could I see you for a moment?"

The other guys at my table, especially Frank, turned pale. We had been joking about the previous night's direct water-balloon hit on a fat lady and her poodle. It was a stupid, dangerous act, but luckily nobody got hurt. We were celebrating our escape from punishment when the chaperone asked to see me.

"Clifton," she began, "do you know about the Mason-Dixon line?"

"No," I said, wondering what this had to do with drenching fat ladies.

"Before the Civil War," she explained, "the Mason-Dixon line was originally the boundary between Maryland and Pennsylvania—the dividing line between the slave and free states." Having escaped one disaster I could feel another brewing. I noticed that her eyes were damp and her hands shaking.

"Today," she continued, "the Mason-Dixon line is a kind of invisible border between the North and the South. When you cross that invisible line out of Washington, D.C., into Maryland, things change."

There was an ominous drift to this conversation, but I wasn't following it. Why did she look and sound so nervous?

"Glen Echo Amusement Park is in Maryland," she said at last, "and the management doesn't allow Negroes inside." She stared at me in silence.

I was still grinning and nodding when the meaning finally sank in. "You mean I can't go to the park," I stuttered, "because I'm a Negro?"

She nodded slowly. "I'm sorry, Clifton," she said, taking my hand. "You'll have to stay in the hotel tonight. Why don't you and I watch a movie on television?"

I walked to the elevators feeling confusion, disbelief, anger and a deep sadness. "What happened, Clifton?" Frank said when I got back to the room. "Did the fat lady tell on us?"

Without saying a word, I walked over to my bed, lay down and began to cry. Frank was stunned into silence. Junior-high boys didn't cry, at least in front of each other.

It wasn't just missing the class adventure that made me feel so sad. For the first time in my life, I was learning what it felt like to be a "nigger." Of course there was discrimination in the North, but the color of my skin had never officially kept me out of a coffee shop, a church—or an amusement park.

"Clifton," Frank whispered, "what is the matter?"

"They won't let me go to Glen Echo Park tonight," I sobbed.

"Because of the water balloon?" he asked.

"No," I answered, "because I'm a Negro."

"Well, that's a relief!" Frank said, and then he laughed, obviously relieved to have escaped punishment for our caper with the balloons. "I thought it was serious!"

Wiping away the tears with my sleeve, I stared at him. "It is serious. They don't let Negroes into the park. I can't go with you!" I shouted. "That's pretty damn serious to me."

I was about to wipe the silly grin off Frank's face with a blow to his jaw when I heard him say, "Then I won't go either."

For an instant we just froze. Then Frank grinned. I will never forget that moment. Frank was just a kid. He wanted to go to that amusement park as much as I did, but there was something even more important than the class night out. Still, he didn't explain or expand.

The next thing I knew, the room was filled with kids listening to Frank. "They don't allow Negroes in the park," he said, "so I'm staying with Clifton."

"Me too," a second boy said.

"Those jerks," a third muttered. "I'm with you, Clifton." My heart began to race. Suddenly, I was not alone. A pint-sized revolution had been born. The "water-balloon brigade," 11 white boys from Long Island, had made its decision: "We won't go." And as I sat on my bed in the center of it all, I felt grateful. But, above all, I was filled with pride.

Dondré Green's story brought that childhood memory back to life. His golfing teammates, like my childhood friends, had an important decision to make. Standing by their friend would cost them dearly. But when it came time to decide, no one hesitated. "Let's get out of here," one of them whispered.

> "It goes to show that there are always good people who will not give in to bigotry. The kind of love they showed me that day will conquer hatred every time."

"They just turned and walked toward the van," Dondré told us. "They didn't debate it. And the younger players joined us without looking back."

Dondré was astounded by the response of his friends—and the people of Louisiana. The whole state was outraged and tried to make it right. The Louisiana House of Representatives proclaimed a Dondré Green Day and passed legislation permitting lawsuits for damages, attorneys' fees and court costs against any private facility that invites a team, then bars any member because of race.

As Dondré concluded, his eyes glistened with tears. "I love my coach and my teammates for sticking by me," he said. "It goes to show that there are always good people who will not give in to bigotry. The kind of love they showed me that day will conquer hatred every time."

Suddenly, the banquet crowd was standing, applauding Dondré Green.

My friends, too, had shown that kind of love. As we sat in the hotel, a chaperone came in waving an envelope. "Boys!" he shouted. "I've just bought 13 tickets to the Senators-Tigers game. Anybody want to go?"

The room erupted in cheers. Not one of us had ever been to a professional baseball game in a real baseball park.

On the way to the stadium, we grew silent as our driver paused before the Lincoln Memorial. For one long moment, I stared through the marble pillars at Mr. Lincoln, bathed in that warm, yellow light. There was still no smile and no sign of hope in his sad and tired eyes.

"*. . . we here highly resolve . . . that this nation, under God, shall have a new birth of freedom . . .*"

In his words and in his life, Lincoln had made it clear that freedom is not free. Every time the color of a person's skin keeps him out of an amusement park or off a country-club fairway, the war for freedom begins again. Sometimes the battle is fought with fists and guns, but more often the most effective weapon is a simple act of love and courage.

Whenever I hear those words from Lincoln's speech at Gettysburg, I remember my 11 white friends, and I feel hope once again. I like to imagine that when we paused that night at the foot of his great monument, Mr. Lincoln smiled at last. As Dondré said, "The kind of love they showed me that day will conquer hatred every time."

No Medals for Joe

By Mayo Simon

The tragic sight of the battleship *Arizona* burning after the attack on Pearl Harbor is etched in our national memory. But fewer remember the *Oklahoma*, another battleship hit on December 7, 1941. A television producer asked me to write a film script about it, and eventually I managed to track down the phone number of someone who, I was told, might have been an eyewitness. When I called, he said in an accent I could not place: "Nobody knows this story. Not my wife, not my children. Come on up, I tell you everything. I remember everything."

The December sun was barely edging over the horizon when Joe Bulgo, a 21-year-old shipyard worker, walked through the gates of Honolulu's Pearl Harbor Navy Yard. It was Sunday morning, so the big shop buildings and repair basin were nearly deserted. Beyond them lay the entire Pacific Battleship Fleet, peacefully at anchor.

Joe had come to this base from a pineapple plantation on the island of Maui, where he was born. At six feet, with broad shoulders and thick arms, he seemed never to tire, and never complained. He would do any job, anytime. After all, he had

48

taken an oath to do what the Navy said.

Today his orders were to caulk and test a new sea valve on the destroyer *Shaw*. He changed into his work clothes and picked up his pneumatic hammer, the biggest one made. When other workers tried to use this chipping gun, it would fly out of their hands. But Joe could hold it. On his way to the vessel, he heard a ship's band playing "The Star-Spangled Banner" for the morning flag-raising.

Then a familiar drone filled the sky. When Joe saw waves of aircraft flying in formation across the harbor, he assumed it was an Army exercise. He thought, *I didn't know we had that many planes.* But within seconds, plumes of water began kicking up among the ships, and he saw the planes' insignia: the rising sun.

Pandemonium broke loose, and Joe ran for cover. Screaming planes swooped low, bombing and strafing the docks and harbor. The *Shaw* rose up in a fiery cloud, its bow blown off. Torpedoes shuddered into the *Oklahoma*; the *Arizona* exploded. Ship after ship—destroyers, cruisers, minelayers—turned over and sank.

After two hours of hell, the invaders vanished, leaving behind an eerie silence—and unbelievable destruction. All the workers were enraged. They wanted to fight back, but had nothing to fight back with. Eventually Joe received new orders.

"Get down to the dock with your chipping outfit," a supervisor shouted to him. "They want you on the *Oklahoma!*"

A launch took him across the channel. Half obscured by black clouds of smoke, battleships were settling to the bottom of the harbor. Hundreds of bodies floated in the water. The *Arizona* was burning, huge flames engulfing its twisted superstructure.

The *Oklahoma* was unrecognizable. All that was left of the huge ship was a curving piece of hull sticking out of the water. It looked like a stranded gray whale.

Standing on the hull under the smoky sky were the chipping gang from Shop 11 and Joe's boss, Julio DeCastro. "Come on," he yelled at Joe. "Let's get going!"

49

At least three torpedoes had capsized the *Oklahoma*, DeCastro told Joe. Its masts were stuck in the mud at the bottom of the harbor, and some 400 sailors were still inside. "Listen," DeCastro said. Joe could hear the trapped sailors tapping on the steel beneath his feet.

The workers tried to cut into the hull with their chipping guns, but it was hard going. "Chipping guns were not made to cut through steel this thick," Joe finally told DeCastro. "Why not burn them out?"

DeCastro showed him an open black patch in the hull. Before he arrived, the burner gang from a Navy ship had tried using acetylene torches. A cork-lined compartment had been set afire, and two trapped sailors had suffocated. "We have no choice," said DeCastro.

Joe started up his gun with an earsplitting clatter. He leaned into the bulkhead, made two cuts and helped bend out a patch. Then he went down into the ship and relieved several exhausted workers chipping at a deck inside.

It was boiling hot. No air. They kept looking for a way to get to the trapped men. But the ship was upside down, and it was impossible to figure where they were. As they drilled, they hit oil tanks, waste tanks, dead ends, and would have to plug up and start over. They knew that, little by little, they were letting out all the ship's trapped air—the only thing keeping the water level down. The more holes they made, the closer the men were to drowning.

Joe worked tirelessly, opening bulkhead after bulkhead, only to find himself in a maze of tiny compartments filled with debris. Sometimes he came upon smashed bodies of sailors in passageways, but he had to keep going.

Whenever Joe paused, he could hear desperate tapping reverberating through the ship. *Save me, save me,* the terrified sailors were saying. *Give me life. . . .* That sound would live in Joe's marrow forever.

Night fell, and the clatter of the chipping guns continued. Fully expecting another Japanese attack, the workers could not use lights on the hull. Instead, they relied on the grisly illumination from the burning *Arizona*.

Toward midnight, when Joe cut into the hull, water bubbled out. He tasted it: sweet. He had hit a freshwater tank. DeCastro found a pump, and after several agonizing hours, they had removed enough water so they could crawl into the tank.

They drilled open its bottom, and a shout went up: inside was a dry, white shaft. *A way in!*

As the others unreeled the hose of his pneumatic hammer, Joe cautiously slid into the shaft with only a cage lantern to light his way. Deeper and deeper he went past the ribs of the upside-down ship. He felt like Jonah in the belly of the whale.

Suddenly the ship began to sway and groan. Joe's stomach tightened in terror. *If it starts to settle, I'm gone.* Fighting the urge to turn back, he tried to catch his breath in the choking stench of oil and sewage.

Then he heard the tapping. Faint. Steady. Joe tapped back with his chisel on the sweating metal bulkhead. *Come on,* he thought. *Tell me where you are.* Finally, answering taps. Joe slid down farther and cocked his head, listening hard. He called for help from DeCastro. The two lifted open a manhole cover, and Joe slipped into an empty compartment. He heard the sound once more. *Tap tap tap.* It was coming from the other side of the bulkhead.

Joe tapped again. Suddenly voices were shouting: "Hurry! Water's coming up!"

Joe's chipping gun dug into the steel with an angry clatter. When trapped air came out with a *whoosh,* the sailors tried to stop it with their fingers. "Don't do that!" Joe yelled. "I'm going to cut it fast." He was a good worker, but he'd never cut so rapidly in his life.

Water was rising to Joe's waist now. But he refused to be

distracted from his work. *Keep on going,* he told himself. *Get them out.*

After cutting three sides, Joe was able to pry open the steel. Immediately the sailors came out in a huge rush of water—kids smeared with oil, hardly able to move or breathe after being trapped for over 20 hours. None had the strength to get to the hatch. So Joe said, "Here, up on my back!"

One by one they climbed on his broad back, and he lifted them to the hatch, where other workers pulled them to safety. By the time the last sailor got out, the water was up to Joe's neck. He scrambled up his hose line, and DeCastro sealed the hatch behind him.

Joe blinked in the sunlight, filling his lungs with fresh air. The sailors, wrapped in blankets, were already in the launch that was taking them to the hospital ship. Joe shouted and waved, but they were too far away to hear. He watched them disappear across the gray harbor.

All told, more than 400 died in the sunken ship; but over four days and nights, Joe Bulgo and the rest of the chipping gang saved 32 men. Later that year, Navy citations "for heroic work with utter disregard of personal safety" were awarded to Joe Bulgo, Julio DeCastro and 18 others from Shop 11.

After the war, Joe married, had four children and joined the merchant marine. During the Vietnam war, he returned to work for the Navy on a chipping gang at the San Francisco Bay Naval Shipyard. When his family said he was working too hard, he'd reply, "Our boys are over there dying. They need these ships."

In 1971, he had his first heart attack. After a second attack, he retired.

The most precious thing he owned, his citation, was lost when somebody stole his suitcase in a bus station. He wrote letter after letter to Washington. He finally got a copy of the citation, with a letter saying he might have a medal coming. He waited, wrote more letters. Nothing happened. It seemed the rescue was a forgotten episode about a forgotten ship.

That was the story Joe Bulgo told me in 1986 when I turned up at his door, 45 years after Pearl Harbor. I kept thinking to myself: *This man deserves a medal. Well, if nothing else, the film will give him and his fellow shipyard workers the recognition they merit.*

But the film was never made, the idea shelved by the network. Discouraged, I put everything away—the script, my notes, the documents, the reminiscences of sailors—and I went on to something else.

Almost a year later, I got a call from Al Ellis of the *U.S.S. Oklahoma* Association, an organization for everyone who had ever served on the ship. Would I speak at their next convention in San Jose?

I was about to politely decline when I remembered something Joe had told me. At the end of the interview, he had said, "You know, I never seen any of those boys I saved. It was all in the dark and so quick. I wish I could have talked with them once."

On May 16, 1987, I waited in the San Jose hotel, where 200 ex-sailors and their wives were meeting. I knew Joe was coming—his wife, Val, had told me how excited he was to have been invited—but I also knew he was ill. Bone cancer, she had said.

Even so, when Val and their daughter, Linda, brought Joe into the big convention room, I was shocked. He was in a wheelchair. His once-powerful body had shrunk. His eyes were filled with pain. "How you doing, Joe?" I said. He pulled my head down and whispered, "Thinking about this night is what's kept me alive."

They seated the Bulgo family in front of the head table. A Navy chaplain gave the invocation. We ate. The master of ceremonies told jokes. Then a band started to play, and everyone was laughing, drinking, dancing. Joe sat stiffly in his chair, his food untouched. I wondered, *Will people actually want to listen to an old war story?*

Finally they introduced me, and I began to speak. I told

them one sailor's story from that dark December day at Pearl Harbor. How he and ten others had been trapped in a compartment slowly filling with water. How for 27 hours they'd banged frantically against the bulkhead, hoping—praying—that someone might save them. And how, finally, a young worker had cut through the bulkhead, releasing them all. I described how the rescuer, in the accent of the islands, had said to the sailors, "Here, on my back"—and then lifted each one to safety.

The crowd was quiet as I read off the names of the sailors rescued that day. "I know three of those men are here tonight. And I also know you never got a chance to thank him. So if there's something you'd like to say to that Hawaiian kid who risked his life to save yours 46 years ago—well, he's right over there."

It is impossible to describe the emotions that swept the hall as I pointed to Joe, and 200 people rose to their feet, cheering. He covered his face with his napkin. He didn't want them to see him crying. Then three elderly veterans embraced the man who could no longer stand, even to acknowledge the applause, but on whose broad, strong back they had once been carried.

Joe Bulgo died two months later. When the San Francisco *Examiner* called me, I told them what I knew. His obituary begins: "Joseph Bulgo, Jr., a neglected hero of Pearl Harbor . . . ."

Well, yes—there hadn't been any medals for Joe. But, I thought to myself, in the end we made things right. We said thank you, at last, to an American hero.

How a simple school memento
came to mean as much as life itself

Friends of the Ring

By Barbara Bressi-Donohue

The day I turned 16, I discovered something about my father that changed our relationship forever. We were living in Mechanicsburg, Pa., that summer in 1965, and Mom, Dad and I had just finished a quiet family birthday celebration.

When my father got up from the dinner table, he called me into his study. "Sit down," he said. "You're old enough to drive now, old enough to understand a couple of things." Then he gave me a handful of papers, which I could see were filled with his handwriting.

"I want you to read this so you know where your roots are. Not everything you inherit is through blood." He sat down opposite me and waited while I read.

I quickly discovered that he'd given me a seven-page manuscript he'd written just after he returned from his service in World War II. I'd heard bits and pieces about his wartime experiences over the years, but he never talked much about them, especially with me. What I knew was that Arthur Anthony Bressi enlisted in 1940 and was captured by the Japanese on Corregidor in 1942.

During 40 months as a prisoner of war in Japanese camps, he had suffered in ways I couldn't comprehend, and the diseases that ravaged his body then—dysentery, malaria, beriberi, pellagra, scurvy—continued to plague him. He still had nightmares, but he had made peace with the world and himself, and had become a renowned advocate of veteran's rights.

He was my hero. But nothing he had told me so far, and certainly nothing in my golden, perfect childhood, prepared me for what he'd written.

"By all the rules, Skinner was a dead man," began the story. "I stood at the wire fence at the Japanese prisoner-of-war camp on Luzon and watched my boyhood buddy, caked in filth and wracked with the pain of multiple diseases, totter toward me. He was dead, only his boisterous spirit hadn't yet left his body. I wanted to look away but couldn't. His blue eyes, watery and dulled, locked on me and wouldn't let go."

Dad and Uncle Skinner—Howard William Ayres—had been fast buddies all through school in Mount Carmel, Pa. They played hooky together, roamed the nearby mountains together and double-dated together. After graduation they enlisted in the Army and rode the same troopship to the Philippines. Skinner was on Bataan when it fell to the Japanese in April 1942. Dad was captured a month later.

> **Then, out of the barracks, tottering slowly, painfully, came the wreckage of a human body. Dad didn't recognize him at first.**

Through the prisoner grapevine, Dad heard about the infamous Bataan Death March. At one of the camps, up to 400 prisoners from Bataan were dying daily, and Dad lost hope of ever seeing his childhood friend again. Then one day he learned that Skinner was at a camp nearby, in the "sick side."

To ask to visit another camp was to ask for a bayonet in the stomach. So Dad volunteered for work detail, hoping his crew would pass through Skinner's camp one day. It did.

"Could I visit the sick side?" he asked the Japanese guards. They gave him a white flag mounted on a bamboo pole, and a pass.

"Walk slowly," they said. "Carry the flag high or be shot. Carry the pass high in the other hand or be clubbed."

The sick side was divided into two sections: one for those expected to recover, and the Zero Ward for those expected to die. Skinner was in the Zero Ward.

Leaning against the barbed-wire fence enclosing the barracks, Dad called out his friend's name. He waited while other prisoners relayed the name. Then, out of the barracks, tottering slowly, painfully, came the wreckage of a human body. Dad didn't recognize him at first.

"Artie," rasped the emaciated body. Skinner fell against the fence and grasped it with both hands to keep from falling.

When last they'd seen each other, Skinner packed a solid 214 pounds. Now his skin was drawn tight over a skeleton that weighed 79 pounds. He was in agony from malaria, amoebic dysentery, pellagra, scurvy and beriberi. For a while his captors fed him burned rice and charcoal in a futile effort to halt the dysentery. But now he couldn't eat or drink for the pain in his mouth and throat. He couldn't wash himself, and no guard would; he was covered with scabs.

It was midafternoon—quiet, hot, with the sun glowing in a cloudless sky. My father was allowed only five minutes with Skinner, and that time was nearly up. Dad fingered the heavy knot of the kerchief tied around his neck. Inside the knot he had hidden his greatest treasure, a simple high school class ring. During his senior year Dad worked for months at odd jobs to earn the $8.75 it cost to buy the ring. The day he graduated, he dashed up to Skinner to show it to him. He was so proud of that ring, he swore he would never part with it. When he was captured, he hid the ring in his kerchief at risk of severe punishment. It was Dad's link to better times, to a better world. The ring was helping to sustain him.

As he stood by the fence, his heart was pounding. His eyes darted around. No guards were in sight. Quickly he unslipped the knot and passed the ring through the fence. "It's yours now, Skinner," he said. "Maybe you can wheel and deal it for something."

"Artie," Skinner replied, trying to pass the ring back. "You ought to hang on to this. You'll need it someday yourself, to wheel and deal."

My father refused to take it back. He had already picked up dysentery, malaria and beriberi and had lost about 20 pounds, but he didn't know then how much worse his condition would get. Six months later, press-ganged into working on an airstrip near Manila, Dad broke down physically. He was sent to a sick ward, where he hung on until the war ended.

All through those painful months he thought about his friend, wondering whether there was the smallest chance he'd survived. He was afraid he knew the answer.

But Skinner hung on. After my father's visit he returned to his sleeping area and hid the ring under the floor so inspection parties would not find it.

A few weeks earlier, one of the guards who patrolled Zero Ward had seemed to take pity on Skinner.

"*Dame,*" the guard said, looking him over. Very bad. Then he dropped half a cigarette and a match alongside the fence.

The day after my father's visit, Skinner took one of the biggest risks of his captivity. He decided to trust the guard. He made a signal and passed him the ring through the fence.

"*Ichi-ban?*" asked the guard. Is it valuable?

Of great value, Skinner replied. He told the guard he wanted to trade it for anything that might help him survive.

The guard, a middle-aged fellow who displayed a prominent gold tooth on the rare occasions when he smiled, paused. "Where did you get it?" he demanded.

Skinner shrugged. "*Tomodachi.*" From a friend.

Quickly the guard slipped the ring into a pocket and left.

One day soon after, the guard dropped something, then strode off on patrol. Skinner picked up a small packet. Inside were sulfanilamide tablets. The guard visited again and again. Each time he brought something. A small basket of limes to combat scurvy, a pair of pants and a jacket, bananas, pickled radishes, canned beef.

> **Skinner knew that the guard would have been shot if his acts of kindness were discovered.**

Further visits brought khaki shorts, a shirt, shoes, a neckerchief and the "damnedest hat ever." Once, the guard dropped 20 packs of cigarettes. Skinner wheeled and dealed these with other prisoners for rice.

Skinner could eat now and retain what went down. The limes, three days after he began eating them, had healed the sores in his mouth sufficiently to enable him to chew food. Soon he was strong enough to bathe.

The guard, arrogant when superiors were in the vicinity, grew friendlier when unobserved. He didn't like war, he told Skinner. He talked about the United States, his family and home. He grinned a gold-toothed smile and showed off pictures of his wife and daughter.

Skinner knew that the guard would have been shot if his acts of kindness were discovered. Neither my dad nor Uncle Skinner ever found out what became of that brave Japanese soldier.

Three weeks after Dad passed his prized ring through the fence, Skinner was on his feet. After three months he was moved to the well side of the camp. There he got better rations. Once his weight went up to a bearable 125 pounds, he asked for a work detail.

When the Philippines was finally liberated, Dad learned that Uncle Skinner had survived the war. Both men returned home to Mount Carmel.

One day, soon after their arrival, Skinner came over for a visit.

"Art," he said, struggling to repress his tears, "as far as I know, I'm the only American who ever left the Zero Ward alive. You remember when you left me at the fence? No man ever looked at me the way you did, and I pray to God no one ever does again. Your eyes said, I'll never see old Skinner alive again."

> ". . . I didn't do anything that another human being wouldn't have done."

Skinner fumbled in his pocket and brought out a little box. Dad's heart quickened, for he knew immediately what was in it. It held an exact copy of his high school ring.

Skinner looked out the window, his face haunted with memory. "That ring, Artie, you. . . it. . . saved my life. I promised I'd get you a new one. There it is."

Then the irrepressible Skinner, the kid who could think up countless ways to play hooky, suddenly laughed. "And see that you don't lose it, buddy! I had to shell out $17.50 for it."

When I finished reading my father's story, I went and sat on his lap and hugged him and wept. I told him how much I loved him and how proud I was of him. Eventually he went to his desk and took out a little gray jewelry box. There, nestled between folds of white velvet, lay the ring. I picked it up in wonder. The initials A.A.B. were inscribed on the inside. A ruby was set into the outside rim, surrounded by the words *Mount Carmel High School* and the date, 1938.

"This is your heritage," he said. His voice was tight with emotion. "I am not a hero. I didn't do anything that another human being wouldn't have done."

My father gave me the ring when I graduated the following year. I wore it when I got married and, a few years later, when my daughter was born. She was premature, and in the first days of her life while she was struggling to live, the ring helped me draw on my own reservoir of courage. Many years later it helped me find the strength to deliver the eulogy at my beloved father's funeral.

Dad died on Veterans Day, 1989, and ever since, our family has memorialized that day with a special, private ritual. When November 11 dawns, I go to my jewelry box and slip a somewhat tarnished high school class ring onto the middle finger of my right hand. Then my husband, Bob, a Vietnam vet, and I fetch the American flag that we keep in our bedroom closet. Outside our tan stucco house, Bob sets a ladder against the wall and gently unfurls the three-by-five-foot flag from its traditional folded triangle. It's a quiet moment for us as he attaches the grommets on the flag to hooks under the overhang, spreading the Stars and Stripes out over the front wall of the house.

At the close of the holiday, I return the ring to its box. And there it sits, waiting for the day when I will pass it down to my daughter, Kim—a reminder of her grandfather, and of the courage and compassion we all carry within.

For more than a century, a Virginia family has
decorated the grave of one Massachusetts soldier—
and honored the sacrifice that has kept us free

Home of
the Brave

By Henry Hurt

★ ★ ★

Morning had not yet broken when Sgt. Jerome Peirce
was rousted from his slumber under the black skies
of the Virginia countryside. His fitful rest had come
on cold, wet ground south of Fredericksburg. But in his mind
was an image so warm that for a moment it melted his bleak
surroundings. Five hundred miles to the north, in Massachusetts,
slept his wife, Albinia, 29, and their little girl, Lucy, who was four.
Peirce had not seen them for nearly two years.

What lay ahead for Jerome Peirce, 33, and his 36th Regiment
Massachusetts Volunteers on this day, May 12, 1864, was one of
the longest and deadliest battles of the Civil War. Well before
dawn, Peirce and his regiment moved forward through "a curtain
of gray mist that enshrouded the earth as with a pall," according
to a fellow Volunteer.

Their destination was a point near the Spotsylvania
Courthouse where Gen. Robert E. Lee's troops had established
a powerful position. One of Lee's aims was to stop the forces of
Gen. Ulysses S. Grant from getting closer to the capital in
Richmond, only 50 miles to the south.

Neither Grant, nor Lee nor Sgt. Peirce, a chairmaker by trade, could imagine what lay ahead. Into a bloody maelstrom—wet, cold, and hungry, his mind filled with images of his wife and daughter—marched Sgt. Peirce.

For those who have never fought, understanding the boldness of the special breed of men who march into battle is a challenge. George Washington's troops had this spirit at the Battle of Saratoga, as did those who fought in the Argonne Forest in the First World War, the men who landed on Iwo Jima in the Second, and at Inchon in Korea—and their sons who poured their lives into Vietnam.

The warriors who fought in the Civil War were as brave as any in history, with this difference: Americans fought and killed each other. The loss of American life in that war—more than 600,000—was greater than in all others put together.

The Civil War was conceivably the most profound threat the United States has ever faced. Had the issue of preserving the Union not been settled so irrevocably, division would have plagued the restored nation, and the country would never have been so strong. Subsequent wars for liberty could have been lost. The men who fought the Civil War believed with passion and fought with fury and when it was finally over, no one could question the inviolability of the Union.

On that early May morning, Sgt. Peirce and his regiment descended into a swampy thicket and then slogged through mud and rain toward a rolling meadow. There Confederate troops were massed at a sharp angle in a line of breastworks and trenches.

As the men marched forward, the din of battle resounded on every side. "Clubbed muskets and bayonets were used freely, as the rain poured down in sheets and the trenches ran red with blood," historian Joseph P. Cullen wrote. "The wounded and dying of both sides were trampled into the mud to drown or suffocate."

Col. Horace Porter of Grant's staff called it "probably the most desperate engagement in the history of modern warfare.

Rank after rank was riddled by shot and shell and bayonet-thrusts, and finally sank, a mass of torn and mutilated corpses; then fresh troops rushed madly forward to replace the dead. Trees were cut completely in half by the incessant musketry fire."

Jerome Peirce's regiment was given the order to charge into this cauldron of horror. "Rising to their feet in the midst of the awful fire, with an alacrity of courage beyond this feeble praise," according to a fellow soldier, the men rushed toward the enemy.

"By early afternoon," according to historian Ed Raus, "the deafening roar of battle could not drown out the hellish shrieks and screams of the wounded. The bullets seemed to fill the air as thick as raindrops." At some point during this carnage, which came to be known as the Battle of the Bloody Angle, a bullet ripped through the heart of Sgt. Jerome Peirce.

After 23 hours, silence settled over the bloody field. Col. Porter wrote that the dead "were piled upon each other in some places four layers deep. Below the mass of fast-decaying corpses, the convulsive twitching of limbs and the writhing of bodies showed that there were wounded men still alive and struggling to extricate themselves from their horrid entombment."

Jerome Peirce's body was shoveled into a hastily dug grave that was then crudely marked, his name scratched on a scrap of wood—probably the lid of an ammunition box. Soon enough, in far-off Massachusetts, death's dark sadness reached Albinia and little Lucy.

The Jaquith family of Billerica, Massachusetts, has sent men to virtually every American conflict, including the Revolutionary War. Today, the family lives in the same house that it occupied in 1665. Its current owner, Lt. Col. Peter Jaquith Casey, fought as a company commander in Vietnam.

It was to this house, to her own family, that Albinia Jaquith Peirce retreated with daughter Lucy. Widowed at 29, Albinia did not marry again. She lived out her years in the family house and died there in 1920 at the age of 85.

Lucy grew up in the old house and became a teacher and librarian. Never marrying, Lucy kept up a warm relationship with her Peirce and Jaquith cousins until she died in 1946 at the age of 87—the last of Jerome Peirce's direct family line.

While the sacrifice of Jerome Peirce is clear, that of Albinia and Lucy is more subtle. Albinia's half-century of loneliness—of wondering what her life might have been if Jerome had lived—is hard to fathom. And Lucy's? Would her life have been different if her father had lived to love her and guide her and nurture her confidence?

She no doubt found sustenance in the treasured letters from her father, who wrote home from major battles all over the South, often sending her flowers from the field. These lines may have stood out: "How much Papa wants to lead you by the hand in some of your pretty summer walks, but he cannot yet. But there is a Good Being who takes care of Pap, Mama and little Lulu and all people."

The nobility of these two women—and countless millions like them—is as important to the soul of our country as the lives of their men who fell on the battlefields.

Several years after the Battle of Bloody Angle, Andrew Birdsall, superintendent of the National Cemetery at Fredericksburg and a Union veteran, received a letter from a Massachusetts family. They asked him to try to locate the field grave of one Jerome Peirce and reinter his remains at the Fredericksburg National Cemetery.

Such requests were common, but this family also enclosed $100 and asked that Jerome Peirce's grave be decorated regularly— so that he not be forgotten.

Superintendent Birdsall opened an account in the Farmers and Merchants Bank of Fredericksburg. He then located Jerome Peirce's grave and moved it to Marye's Heights, a Confederate stronghold converted into the National Cemetery. Birdsall enlisted his own family—including his four daughters who would all marry Southerners—to see that the Peirce grave got special decorations at appropriate times.

The final resting place of Jerome Peirce was marked by a small stub of a stone. It is one of 15,000 graves on that hillside. And he was one of more than 600,000 men killed in that war more than 130 years ago. Was it possible that this soldier with no living descendants could be remembered by strangers in a land where he was the enemy?

In an early May in the 1990s, a 90-year-old Virginian, Alice Heflin Abernathy, fretted about whether she would be able to get out to the Fredericksburg National Cemetery to put flowers on Jerome Peirce's grave. "He was always just Jerome to us," says Mrs. Abernathy, a diminutive and stately woman with a firm voice and piercing eyes. "We never really knew anything about him except that his family sent my grandfather $100 and asked us to take care of his grave. It was our duty, so that's what we've done."

When she was little, Alice Heflin went to the cemetery with her parents to decorate the grave of this Union soldier. Later, she went with her husband—then, still later, either with her nieces or alone.

The original $100 account is still in a local bank, showing small withdrawals of the interest over the years. The balance now stands at $173. "We didn't really use the money much," says Mrs. Abernathy. "Pretty flowers in the garden or from the fields were just as nice for Jerome." Over the years, the cemetery caretakers often wondered about the special decorations that would appear on the single grave.

Then, one Memorial Day, Alice Abernathy decided she was not able to climb the steep hill to decorate Jerome's grave. So she sent her great nephew, Kent Ingalls, then 11, the great, great grandson of Andrew Birdsall. Kent was thrilled with his mission and told his school class about it. Soon it was reported in the newspaper.

Meanwhile, in Billerica, Mass., the news that the grave in

Virginia was regularly decorated by a Southern family sent Colonel Casey to the attic of the Jaquith house. There he discovered photographs and letters that reflected Albinia's and Lucy's quiet presence in the family. This set him to wondering whether even more answers might come from the old graveyard a few hundred yards from the Jaquith house.

One wintery Saturday morning, Casey and his son, Seth, trudged through the snow to take a look. Soon, they spotted the name Peirce across the top of one of the grave markers. They brushed away the snow. The marker is large—more than three feet across—and prominently inscribed upon it is the name of Jerome Peirce along with his military affiliation, where he was killed and where he is buried. There also are the names and dates of Albinia and Lucy—as well as the name of Charles Jerome Pierce, a son born before Lucy who died the day of his birth.

"It was very moving to stand there and think about it all," Casey says. "It's like the whole family is there together." Then a patch of red caught the colonel's eye. He reached down and pulled from the snow an American flag. *Someone must have put it there on Memorial Day*, he thought.

"We must never forget Jerome," Alice Abernathy says. And still, nearly 140 years after Sgt. Peirce died, each Memorial Day, his grave will be honored as usual with the same spirit of respect and reconciliation that has healed the country. He has no direct descendants to honor him as he lies on this peaceful hillside—the eternal home for so many of the brave. Instead, Jerome Peirce left something else: because of his sacrifice, and the sacrifice of so many others to preserve our Union, countless millions the world over live today in freedom.

First, 14-year-old Karen Hartsock fought an
inferno to save the lives of her brother and sisters.
Then she fought to save herself.

The Little Heroine of Castlewood

By Sheldon Kelly

Fire! Fire!

Karen Hartsock, asleep in the dawn hours of June 13, 1982,
thought she was dreaming. Then she heard clearly her father's
desperate shouts as they rang through their old log farmhouse
in the rugged Appalachian foothills of Castlewood, Va.

Fire!

The pretty 14-year-old leaped from her bed and ran to the
hallway. Fire and smoke spurted from the walls; the nearby stairway was almost engulfed in flames. Horrified, she began yelling
for her two younger sisters and brother.

In seconds the upstairs was filled with thick smoke. Eleven-
year-old Norma Kay stumbled from her room, sobbing hysteri-
cally. Karen—barely five feet tall—wrapped her arms around her
sister and pulled her fiercely down the fiery stairway to safety.

While her father—partially invalided from recent open-heart surgery—smothered the flames on Norma Kay's pajamas, Karen fought her way back up the stairs. She knew that 12-year-old Loretta and 9-year-old Johnny—who was crippled by cerebral palsy—would perish if she didn't reach them. "God, help me!" she screamed as her polyester nightgown burst into flames.

Karen turned back toward the wall of fire. "Ree-Ree! Ree-Ree!" She shouted Loretta's nickname, unaware that her sister had escaped earlier.

The walls of the hallway were now fully ablaze. Karen gasped for air, sucking in acrid smoke. As she groped blindly for Johnny's bed, the bedroom wall erupted into flames, lighting the way to her sleeping brother. Frantically wrapping him in a blanket, she carried the youngster into the inferno-like hallway.

The fire now raged along the full length of the stairway, with flames leaping nearly to the ceiling. Muffled explosions shook the house. There was a flash around Karen's head as her long, auburn hair caught fire. Holding Johnny with one arm, she struggled to snuff out the flames, screaming as they burned into her scalp.

Suddenly a section of thick, burning wallpaper toppled onto her head and shoulders. Still holding Johnny with one arm, she knocked it away. Then another section fell, and another! The pain seemed unbearable.

Fearing unconsciousness, Karen tightened her hold around Johnny and rushed down the stairs. Strangely, the pain now began to subside. Indeed, she felt almost euphoric, invincible. Near the bottom of the stairs she saw her father. "Here!" she shouted, heaving her brother with all of her might.

"I've got him!" Claude Hartsock yelled. "Now, you come on!" "Come on!"

Instead, Karen turned back toward the wall of fire. "Ree-Ree! Ree-Ree!" She shouted Loretta's nickname, unaware that her sister had escaped earlier. A second later the banister overhead collapsed, pinning Karen beneath a pile of burning debris.

Claude Hartsock, his weakened heart palpitating wildly, pulled his daughter from underneath the banister and out into the yard. There his wife, Rachel, flung her own body on top of Karen's in an effort to smother the flames. Still, Karen struggled to get up: I have a job to do. I need to get Ree-Ree.

Just then the entire house gushed up in an immense fireball. Karen's older brother, David, who had escaped by climbing down an antenna outside his bedroom window, ran to meet the ambulance he had called. Sobbing, Ree-Ree and Norma Kay knelt with their mother around Karen's charred body. Karen was dying.

> "Please get well, Big Sister. We're all so lonely without you."

At the University of Virginia Hospital Burn Center in Charlottesville, doctors worked feverishly to save the little heroine. Second- and third-degree burns covered more than 80 percent of her body. A tube was inserted in her windpipe to help her breathe. While a respirator pumped oxygen into her lungs, burned portions of her arms, breasts and neck were removed—and all of her fingers amputated. She was given a less than 10 percent chance of surviving.

For days Karen remained in critical condition. The first of many skin grafts—the surgical placing of undamaged skin over a burned area—was performed three days after her admission. During the time it took to heal, her body remained susceptible to deadly bacterial infections. Still, incredibly, she clung to life.

Although heavily sedated, she struggled to remain conscious, calmly enduring her painful treatment. Unable to speak because of the tube in her trachea, her scorched eyes covered with medicated cream and gauze, Karen managed to send messages by mouthing her words, gesturing, and pointing with her splinted, bandaged hands to letters on a card. "I'm fine," she signaled to an incredulous medical staff. "Thank you, thank you!"

One day Karen frantically motioned that she wanted something. After countless questions and signals, the nurses realized that she wanted Ree-Ree. Although she had been told repeatedly that her sister was alive, Karen suddenly feared that she was being spared from the awful truth—that Ree-Ree had perished.

Minutes later Ree-Ree sat beside her, touching her lovingly. "Please get well, Big Sister. We're all so lonely without you." Karen tried to rise, waving her hands gleefully. Almost immediately, her condition began to improve.

Still, recovery would be a painful process. Twice daily she was taken to the "tank room" for debriding—the removal of dead skin with tweezers and scissors—considered by many doctors to be the most painful of all medical procedures. Although sedated with pain-killing drugs, some screaming patients have to be physically restrained as nurses cut and pick, stopping only to wash blood and dead tissue down the tank table's drain.

> "God created you for a special purpose. You've already proved that! You cannot give up now when the beauty of his spirit is beginning to show in you."

Yet even during this horrifying treatment, Karen never faltered. Moaning slightly, her head turned away, she managed to communicate: "I'm okay. I know you don't mean to hurt me. Thank you."

By mid-July, Karen had undergone her second graft. Although her condition had stabilized, it would be weeks before she would be beyond the easy reach of death. Suddenly her persistent struggle to remain conscious intensified; she feared anesthesia, even sleep. She began signaling a desperate message—one that not even her family could interpret. A Baptist minister, Pastor Fred Patrick, joined the bedside vigil, watching the hopeless exchange of questions and signals. Finally he knelt by her side. "Do you want a Bible, Karen?" She nodded. Then for the first time, she was able to speak, in a whisper: "Yes, please."

A Bible was placed next to her pillow. And the minister returned with tape recordings of the Bible. As the first tape began playing, Karen waved her hands ecstatically. And once more doctors noted marked improvement.

Yet a new dimension to Karen's suffering lurked in the future. With her eyes covered, she had been unable to see her face or body. Now, as nurses removed her eye covering, she saw the purplish, twisted stubs where her fingers had been, and her arms covered with thick scar tissue. Then she saw her torso, neck and face. Weeping, she told the nurses, "I want to die."

Karen's condition began to deteriorate. Doctors and nurses tried to console her—to no avail. Even her mother failed to dissuade Karen from wanting death. Hearing the news, Fred Patrick rushed to her room. Karen turned her head, trying to hide her face from the minister. "There's no reason to go on," she whispered, tears streaming down her scarred cheeks.

"You are the bravest person I've ever met," the pastor announced. "God created you for a special purpose. You've already proved that! You cannot give up now when the beauty of his spirit is beginning to show in you." He quoted her a passage from Romans: "And we know that all things work together for good to them that love God, to them who are called according to his purpose."

Karen's tears became tears of joy. The minister had explained exactly what she recalled thinking on the night of the fire! She had had a job to do then. And she had one now.

Karen's will to survive came back even stronger than before. Someday, somehow, she told her family cheerfully, she would fulfill her childhood dream of becoming a nurse.

On August 4—52 days after the fire—Karen's name was removed from the critical list. Several weeks later she was transferred to a rehabilitation center, where she began rigorous therapy treatment and resumed her high-school studies. Although she had undergone eight major skin grafts and was scheduled to receive many more, plus reconstructive surgery, she felt happy. Her hair was growing back; she could walk unassisted; her voice—although it would remain hoarse—was stronger, her vision clear.

On March 20, 1983, after eight months of intensive therapy and hundreds of operations, Karen was released. The entire family was waiting to take her home to a newly rented farmhouse in the familiar Appalachian foothills. Offers of free treatment from several hospitals were kindly rejected. Karen wished to remain close to her loved ones—especially her father, who had been recently told that he had terminal lung cancer. Together, she vowed to him, they would fight off the pain.

> **"I don't think of myself as a hero-ine," she said. "I just love my family."**

Dressed in elasticized material—a tight-fitting garment covering her arms, torso and face—Karen stayed busy each day giving emotional support to her dying father. Soon the diminutive youngster was once again the family's "big sister," advising, scolding and joking with everyone.

Even as the reconstructive surgery resumed, Karen's cheerful demeanor remained unchanged. Her high-school studies were brought to her each day. She subscribed to nursing magazines, made inquiries about nursing schools and became an outspoken proponent of the rights of the handicapped. Told that she could not return to the local hospital as a volunteer nurse's aide because of her injuries, she asked, "Who knows how to help injured people better than someone who is permanently injured?"

In July, Karen was informed that she had been selected to receive both the Young American Medal for Bravery and the Carnegie Medal for extraordinary heroism. Karen was amazed. "I don't think of myself as a heroine," she said. "I just love my family." She continued to assist her father between her own agonizing bouts with pain. And on September 8, while she sat alone with him, he whispered, "I'm sorry I can't stay and help you keep fighting, honey. I love you." Then he died.

On October 6, 1983, Karen stood on the steps of the White House as President Reagan decorated her for bravery. "I know, Karen, that in one sense your father is not with us today," the President said. "But in another sense, I believe with all my heart he is here. And he's very proud." Several weeks later, she was presented the Carnegie Medal in recognition of an outstanding act of heroism.

Says Dr. Richard Edlich, director of the University of Virginia Emergency Medical Services and Burn Center: "Karen is one of those rare and remarkable individuals who will never surrender; whose selfless love and spiritual belief are in themselves miraculous life-support systems. Her will and resolve are an inspiration to all burn victims. And her incredible heroism is an inspiration to us all."

Abe Lincoln's Glorious Failure

By Philip B. Kunhardt, Jr.
CONDENSED FROM
A New Birth of Freedom: Lincoln at Gettysburg

I f Mary Lincoln had got her way, her husband would never have gone to Gettysburg. The first couple of the land awakened on November 18, 1863, to find their ten-year-old son, Tad, ill. They had lost two of their four children and now Mrs. Lincoln, still dressed in mourning, insisted that her husband stay in Washington. But Lincoln was determined to go. He had something special to say in Pennsylvania, something he hoped would make a difference.

During the first days of July, 51,000 men were killed, wounded or listed as missing in what would prove the decisive Union victory of the Civil War. The anguished cries of the maimed made a wailing, screeching chorus as they were moved to improvised operating tables. "For seven days the tables literally ran blood," wrote a nurse. Wagons were loaded to overflowing with amputated arms and legs, driven off, dumped in a trench. Preachers read the 23rd Psalm over and over as fast as their lips could say it, as soldiers expired.

During this grim aftermath, a national cemetery on the fighting ground was proposed. The consecration commission invited silver-tongued Edward Everett—known for his cultured words and patriotic fervor—to deliver the dedication speech. Everett, a former congressman and governor of Massachusetts, agreed to speak on November 19.

> **When the battle of Gettysburg had begun, he had gone down on his knees and asked God not to let the nation perish. He felt his prayers had been answered.**

In October, Lincoln announced he would attend the ceremonies. This startled the commissioners, who had not expected the President to leave the capital in wartime. Now, how could he not be asked to speak? The thought made them nervous. Lincoln could be indelicate, or go into one of his embarrassing off-the-cuff talks. But it was unthinkable not to ask the President to say something.

On November 2, the commission wrote Lincoln asking him to deliver "a few appropriate remarks." Lincoln must have known that the request was an afterthought. It did not matter. When the battle of Gettysburg had begun, he had gone down on his knees and asked God not to let the nation perish. He felt his prayers had been answered. Now he wanted to sum up what he passionately felt about the nation. He had hardly two weeks to prepare his remarks, but already he had the gist of what he might say. God would help him with the rest.

It was a busy time, yet the speech was rarely out of his mind. He confided to a friend that it was not going smoothly. Then he took off his hat, which he used as a desk drawer, tucking important papers beneath the inner rim, and withdrew a single piece of paper. "Well, there is what I have written for Gettysburg," he said. "It does not suit me, but I have not time for anything more."

Lincoln arrived at Gettysburg the day before the ceremonies.

At a large dinner that evening, Edward Everett was surprised by Lincoln's urbanity. He said later that Lincoln had been "the peer of any person present so far as manners, appearance, and conversation were concerned." But Lincoln did not distinguish himself after dinner when the crowd outside demanded a speech. He told them he had no speech and continued, "In my position, it is important that I should not say any foolish things."

"If you can help it," a voice called from the crowd.

Lincoln excused himself to consider further the few words he was expected to deliver the next day and went to his room. At midnight he received a telegram from his wife: "The doctor has just left. We hope dear Taddie is slightly better." Soon the lights in Lincoln's room were extinguished.

Around nine the next morning, Lincoln copied his address onto two pages and tucked them into his coat pocket. Then he put on his high hat, tugged white gloves over his hands and went downstairs to join the procession of dignitaries. As they passed the blood-soaked fields, scraps of men's lives were everywhere—a dented canteen, a torn picture of a child.

The procession passed through the crowd of 15,000 that had gathered on the grounds of the cemetery. Lincoln was guided to a worn settee on the speakers' platform. He was flanked by Secretary of State William H. Seward and Edward Everett.

The chaplain of the Senate gave the invocation. Shortly afterward, Everett was introduced. At 69, the grand old orator trembled slightly, frightened his mind would go blank during his long, memorized speech; he bowed toward Lincoln and turned to the crowd.

"Standing beneath this serene sky. . . ." The words carried like silver bells, and even the people far away could hear them. Everett knew just when to raise and lower his voice, just what hand movements to make to emphasize a point. Lincoln looked on in fascination.

Everett described how citizens who fell in battle were buried in ancient Athens; then he launched into a long explanation of the war and how it came about, described the battle and predicted that many Southerners were "yearning to see the dear old flag floating upon their capitols. . . ." Finally, after an hour and 57 minutes, he finished, amid enthusiastic applause.

Now Lincoln was introduced. It was 2 P.M.

On the settee, Lincoln turned to Secretary Seward and said nervously, "They won't like it."

The President fitted on his steel spectacles, rose slowly and stepped to the front of the platform. Holding the two pages of his speech in one hand, he looked out over the throng. His left hand moved up his coat and grasped the lapel, his thumb erect. He began to speak.

An outdoor speaker all his life, Lincoln spoke in a high-pitched, almost squeaky voice that carried out over the crowd like the sound of a bugle. He spoke slowly, deliberately, emphasizing the important words. He referred to his written pages only once. He never moved his feet or made any gesture with his hands.

In the beginning his expression was set—serious and sad—but a few sentences into the speech his face came alive. His voice lowered in tone, turning melodious. As he spoke "The world will little note nor long remember," his voice almost broke, but then it was back, strong and clear. The people strained to hear, stood on tiptoe, craned their necks.

> No, this speech could not be dismissed that easily. The strange chemistry that alters events after they have happened was at work.

All of a sudden, Lincoln was finished. His speech had taken about two minutes. Now, some said, there was a burst of applause; others reported dead silence. In any case, the people were bewildered. They had expected something more. And this speech, whatever its length, had been so prayer-like it seemed almost inappropriate to applaud.

Edward Everett turned to the Secretary of State. "What did you think, Mr. Seward?"

"A failure. His speech is not the equal of him," replied Seward.

Everett said some polite words to the President about his address. But Lincoln dismissed him. "I failed; I failed, and that is about all that can be said about it."

As Lincoln sat down, John Russell Young of the *Philadelphia Press* asked, "Is that all?" And the President replied yes, it was.

When the speech was printed in the newspapers, there were some admirers. "Simple and felicitous," one magazine called it. "Brief . . . beautiful . . . inspiring," read one newspaper report. But other papers damned Lincoln, calling his Gettysburg address "an insult to the memory of the dead." At any rate, it was over and could be forgotten.

Or could it? No, this speech could not be dismissed that easily. The strange chemistry that alters events after they have happened was at work. Lincoln's rhythmic words and his themes had already begun to seep into the American fabric. He had spoken just ten sentences. Of his 271 words, 202 of them were just one syllable. How could such primer words become known as one of the greatest utterances in the English language?

It did not happen overnight. The war had to be won. A bullet had to be fired in a theater box. The name of Lincoln had to become synonymous with the freeing of the slaves, with morality and conscience, with a largeness of spirit and a forgiveness of the heart, "with malice toward none; with charity for all."

And Lincoln's "few appropriate remarks" had to age. They had to be memorized and recited by millions of American schoolchildren, had to ring out over the land at innumerable exercises of remembrance, ensuring that the brave men who "gave their lives that [their] nation might live . . . shall not have died in vain," and that their government "shall not perish from the earth."

Only then could the speech take its rightful place in history.

The Gettysburg Address

Four score and seven years ago our fathers brought on this continent a new nation conceived in liberty and dedicated to the proposition that all men are created equal.

Now we are engaged in a great civil war testing whether that nation, or any nation so conceived and so dedicated, can long endure. We are met on a great battle-field of that war. We have come to dedicate a portion of that field as a final resting-place for those who here gave their lives that that nation might live. It is altogether fitting and proper that we should do this.

But, in a larger sense, we cannot dedicate, we cannot consecrate, we cannot hallow this ground. The brave men, living and dead, who struggled here have consecrated it far above our poor power to add or detract. The world will little note nor long remember what we say here, but it can never forget what they did here. It is for us the living rather to be dedicated here to the unfinished work which they who fought here have thus far so nobly advanced. It is rather for us to be here dedicated to the great task remaining before us—that from these honoured dead we take increased devotion to that cause for which they gave the last full measure of devotion—that we here highly resolve that these dead shall not have died in vain, that this nation under God shall have a new birth of freedom, and that government of the people, by the people, for the people, shall not perish from the earth.